ANDREW CLAY

Experience Vancouver Like A Native

Your Ultimate Guide to Vancouver's Bucket List Attractions, Accommodations and Essentials

Contents

About Vancouver

Vancouver is a coastal city located in the Lower Mainland region of British Columbia, Canada. Known for its stunning natural beauty, diverse population, and vibrant cultural scene, Vancouver is consistently ranked among the most livable cities in the world. It is situated between the Pacific Ocean and the Coast Mountain Range, offering a unique blend of urban and outdoor experiences.

Geography and Climate

Vancouver's geography is characterized by its proximity to the ocean and mountains. The city is surrounded by water, including the Burrard Inlet, English Bay, and the Strait of Georgia. To the north, the Coast Mountains provide a dramatic backdrop. The city's moderate climate is influenced by the Pacific Ocean, resulting in mild, rainy winters and warm, dry summers. This climate is conducive to a wide range of outdoor activities year-round. (MORE DETAILS ON THIS IN THE NEXT CHAPTER)

Cultural Diversity

Vancouver is known for its rich cultural diversity. It is a melting pot of ethnicities and languages, with a significant population of immigrants from various parts of the world. This diversity is reflected in the city's cuisine, festivals, and neighborhoods. The city celebrates cultural events like the Vancouver International Film Festival, Chinese New Year, and Diwali, showcasing its global character.

Neighborhoods

Vancouver is composed of a variety of neighborhoods, each with its own distinct character. Downtown Vancouver is the commercial and entertainment hub, with towering skyscrapers, luxury shopping on Robson Street, and entertainment options like theaters and concert venues. The historic Gastown district features cobblestone streets, the famous Gastown Steam Clock, and a mix of boutiques, galleries, and restaurants.

Chinatown, one of the oldest in North America, offers a blend of traditional and modern elements, from herbal shops and markets to contemporary art galleries. Yaletown is a trendy neighborhood known for its converted warehouses, upscale boutiques, and vibrant nightlife.

The West End, located near Stanley Park, is a diverse and densely populated residential area with a relaxed atmosphere, beautiful beaches, and LGBTQ+ friendly spaces. Kitsilano (Kits) is another laid-back area with sandy beaches, outdoor recreational activities, and a bohemian vibe.

Outdoor Activities

Vancouver is renowned for its outdoor recreational opportunities. Stanley Park, a large urban park at the edge of downtown, offers lush gardens, scenic seawall paths, and the Vancouver Aquarium. The Grouse Mountain and Cypress Mountain ski resorts are easily accessible from the city, providing winter sports enthusiasts with opportunities for skiing, snowboarding, and snowshoeing.

The Seawall is a popular waterfront pathway that encircles the downtown peninsula, offering breathtaking views of the ocean, mountains, and city skyline. Locals and visitors alike enjoy biking, walking, jogging, and rollerblading along this picturesque route.

Cultural Attractions

The city boasts numerous cultural attractions, including the Vancouver Art Gallery, which houses an extensive collection of Canadian and Indigenous art, as well as international works. The Museum of Anthropology at the University of British Columbia showcases indigenous art and cultural artifacts from around the world.

Granville Island is a cultural hotspot with a public market, artisan shops, galleries, and theaters. The Vancouver Symphony Orchestra, Vancouver Opera, and various theater companies contribute to the city's thriving arts scene.

Economy

Vancouver's economy is diverse and driven by sectors such as technology, film and television production, tourism, natural resources, and trade. The Port of Vancouver is one of North America's largest and busiest ports, handling a wide range of cargo and facilitating international trade.

Important Tips Before Going

Weather and Climate

Vancouver experiences a mild and temperate climate influenced by its coastal location. The weather can be unpredictable, so packing for different seasons is essential. Here's what you can expect:

- **Spring (March to May):** Spring brings mild temperatures and blossoming flowers. Average highs range from 10°C to 15°C (50°F to 59°F), and rain is common.
- **Summer (June to August):** Summer is warm and pleasant, with average highs ranging from 20°C to 25°C (68°F to 77°F). Rainfall decreases, and outdoor activities are popular.
- **Fall (September to November):** Fall brings cooler temperatures, with average highs ranging from 12°C to 18°C (54°F to 64°F). Rain increases, and the city is adorned with colorful foliage.
- **Winter (December to February):** Winters are mild compared to many other Canadian cities. Average highs range from 5°C to 8°C (41°F to 46°F), and rain is common. Snowfall is infrequent but can occur in higher elevations.

Visa Requirements

Visitors to Canada, including Vancouver, may need a visa or an Electronic Travel Authorization (eTA) to enter the country. Here's what you need to know:

- **eTA:** Most international travelers require an eTA, which is an entry requirement for visa-exempt foreign nationals traveling to Canada by air. Apply for an eTA online before your trip.
- **Visa:** If you're not eligible for an eTA, you'll need a visa to enter Canada. Check with the nearest Canadian consulate or embassy for details and application requirements.
- **Passport:** Ensure your passport is valid for the duration of your stay in Canada.

Traveling Documents

When traveling to Vancouver, it's important to have the following documents:

- **Passport:** A valid passport is required for entry into Canada.
- **eTA:** If required, ensure you have received your approved eTA before boarding your flight.
- **Travel Insurance:** Consider obtaining travel insurance to cover medical emergencies, trip cancellations, and unexpected events.
- **Health Insurance:** It's advisable to have health insurance that covers medical expenses during your stay.
- **Driver's License:** If you plan to rent a car, an international driver's license may be necessary. Check with your rental company.
- **Credit Cards and Cash:** Canadian currency is the Canadian Dollar (CAD), and credit cards are widely accepted. However, it's a good

idea to carry some local currency for small transactions.

- **Itinerary and Reservations:** Have copies of your travel itinerary, hotel reservations, and any tour bookings you've made.
- **Emergency Contacts:** Keep a list of emergency contacts, including the nearest consulate or embassy.

Customs and Entry Regulations:

- Declare any goods you're bringing into Canada, including gifts, purchases, and items for personal use.
- Follow customs regulations regarding prohibited items, medications, and restricted items.

Additional Tips:

- Check the specific requirements for your country of residence before traveling.
- Ensure you have all necessary documents before your departure.
- Keep physical and digital copies of important documents in case of loss or theft.

The Airport

Vancouver International Airport, often referred to as **YVR**, is the main international airport serving Vancouver and the surrounding region. Situated on Sea Island in Richmond, British Columbia, YVR is well-connected to the city and offers a wide range of services, facilities, and transportation options.

Basic Navigation Tips:

1. **Terminal Layout**: YVR consists of three terminals: the International Terminal (Main Terminal), Domestic Terminal, and South Terminal. The International Terminal has several concourses (A, B, C, D, and E), while the Domestic Terminal serves flights within Canada.

2. **Arrival Procedures**: After landing, follow signs to the Immigration and Customs area for international flights or proceed to the baggage claim area for domestic flights.

3. **Ground Transportation**: From the terminals, you can access various ground transportation options, including taxis, ride-sharing services, shuttles, and public transit.

Practical Tips:

1. **Customs and Immigration**: For international travelers, be prepared to complete immigration and customs procedures. Have your passport, travel documents, and customs declaration forms ready.

2. **Baggage Claim**: Locate your baggage carousel based on your flight information. If you have connecting flights, follow the signs for "Connecting Flights" to recheck your baggage.

3. **Currency Exchange**: Currency exchange services are available within the airport. Consider exchanging a small amount for immediate expenses and using ATMs for better exchange rates.

4. **Wi-Fi and Charging**: YVR offers free Wi-Fi throughout the terminals. Look for charging stations to keep your devices powered.

5. **Dining and Shopping**: The airport boasts a variety of dining options and shops, including duty-free shops for international travelers.

Insider Tips:

1. **Pre-Book Parking**: If you're driving to the airport, consider pre-booking your parking spot to secure the best rates and ensure availability.
2. **Security Checkpoints**: Allow enough time for security screening, especially during peak travel hours. Check the YVR website for estimated wait times at security checkpoints.
3. **Lounges**: If you're eligible, access airport lounges for a more relaxed and comfortable pre-flight experience.
4. **Public Art**: YVR is renowned for its impressive collection of public art. Take some time to explore the terminals and appreciate the artwork on display.
5. **Flight Information**: Stay informed about flight details through the airport's digital displays, mobile app, and website.

Transportation:

- **SkyTrain**: The Canada Line SkyTrain connects YVR to Downtown Vancouver and Richmond. The station is easily accessible from both the International and Domestic Terminals.
- **Taxis and Ride-Sharing**: Taxis and ride-sharing services are available curbside at designated areas outside the terminals.
- **Shuttle Services**: Numerous shuttle services provide transportation to various destinations within the city and the surrounding area.

Vancouver International Airport is not only a gateway to the city but also an excellent starting point for exploring Vancouver and the beautiful province of British Columbia. Familiarize yourself with the airport's layout, services, and transportation options to ensure a smooth and enjoyable travel experience.

Complete Bucket List

This complete Bucket List will be your guide when choosing places to visit, to shop and to get the best for yourself

Exploring the Enchanting Stanley Park

Nestled at the heart of Vancouver, Stanley Park stands as an iconic testament to the city's natural beauty and captivating charm. Spanning over 1,000 acres, this urban oasis boasts a harmonious blend of lush forests, stunning waterfront views, and an array of attractions that beckon visitors to immerse themselves in its wonder.

Address and GPS Position: Stanley Park, Vancouver, BC V6G 1Z4, Canada
  GPS Coordinates: 49.301705, -123.141700

As you set foot in Stanley Park, the scent of pine and the gentle rustling of leaves immediately welcome you to a realm of serenity. Begin your journey at the picturesque Totem Poles, standing as cultural guardians at the entrance, each telling stories of Indigenous peoples' history and heritage.

Navigating the Park: *Follow the Seawall:* Embark on a leisurely stroll or rent a bike to traverse the iconic Seawall that hugs the park's perimeter. The path unfolds along the waterfront, revealing stunning vistas of the city skyline, the Lions Gate Bridge, and the vast expanse of the Pacific Ocean.

Lost Lagoon: Venture deeper into the park and encounter the enchanting Lost Lagoon, a haven for swans, ducks, and other waterfowl. Meander along the scenic trails that encircle the lagoon, allowing the tranquil waters to mirror the lush greenery and vibrant blossoms.

Beaver Lake: Escape the urban hustle and venture to Beaver Lake, a secluded gem hidden amidst the trees. Here, you can savor a serene moment by the water's edge or embark on a peaceful hike around the lake's circumference.

Prospect Point: Head northwest and find yourself at Prospect Point, where the stunning Prospect Point Lighthouse presides over the rugged cliffs. Gaze out at the majestic Lions Gate Bridge and the tumultuous waters below, a reminder of the park's coastal majesty.

Stanley Park Pavilion: Retreat to the Stanley Park Pavilion, a charming historic building that houses a delightful restaurant and tea room. Savor delectable cuisine while surrounded by the park's natural splendor.

Tips and Essential Information:

- **Park Hours:** Stanley Park is open year-round, 24 hours a day. However, some attractions may have specific operating hours.
- **Parking:** Limited parking is available within the park, but it can get crowded. Consider using public transportation or biking to the park.
- **Biking:** Rentals are available near the entrance, providing a convenient way to explore the park's trails.
- **Wildlife:** Keep a respectful distance from wildlife and refrain from

feeding them.
- **Weather:** Dress in layers and wear comfortable shoes suitable for walking or biking.
- **Photography:** Capture the breathtaking vistas, lush landscapes, and intricate details that make Stanley Park a photographer's paradise.

Getting There:

- **Public Transit:** Take a TransLink bus from various points in Vancouver to the park's entrance.
- **Biking:** Enjoy a scenic ride along the Seawall from downtown Vancouver.
- **Driving:** If driving, follow the signs from downtown Vancouver to Stanley Park. GPS Coordinates: 49.301705, -123.141700.

Stanley Park, with its awe-inspiring beauty, rich history, and myriad of attractions, stands as a sanctuary for nature lovers, history enthusiasts, and anyone seeking a respite from the urban bustle. As you explore its winding trails and discover its hidden treasures, let the tranquility and grandeur of Stanley Park leave an indelible imprint on your heart and soul.

Grouse Mountain

Nestled majestically in the embrace of Vancouver's North Shore Mountains, Grouse Mountain beckons adventurers to ascend into a world of alpine wonders and breathtaking vistas. This rugged paradise offers an array of year-round activities, making it a playground for outdoor enthusiasts seeking both exhilaration and tranquility.

Address and GPS Position: Grouse Mountain, 6400 Nancy Greene Way, North Vancouver, BC V7R 4K9, Canada
  GPS Coordinates: 49.380069, -123.081401

Ascending to New Heights: Begin your journey by ascending the mountain via the Grouse Mountain Skyride, a state-of-the-art gondola that whisks you from the base to the alpine paradise above. As you soar above the lush forests, anticipation builds for the treasures that await at the summit.

  Year-Round Activities: *Grouse Grind:* For the adventurous souls, the Grouse Grind trail presents an invigorating challenge. Affectionately known as "Mother Nature's Stairmaster," this uphill hike rewards your efforts with stunning panoramic views at the top.

  Skiing and Snowboarding: In the winter months, Grouse Mountain transforms into a winter wonderland with pristine slopes suitable for both beginners and seasoned skiers and snowboarders.

  Eye of the Wind: Visit the Eye of the Wind, a towering wind turbine with an observation deck that provides awe-inspiring views of the surrounding landscape. Peer out over the city of Vancouver, the ocean, and the coastal mountains.

  Wildlife Refuge: Encounter native wildlife at the Grouse Mountain Wildlife Refuge. Marvel at majestic grizzly bears, timber wolves, and owls, learning about their habitat and conservation efforts.

Tips and Essential Information:

- **Mountain Hours:** Grouse Mountain operates year-round with varying hours for different seasons and activities. Check the official website for current information.
- **Dress Accordingly:** Even in summer, temperatures can be cooler at higher altitudes. Dress in layers and wear sturdy footwear

suitable for walking.

- **Sun Protection:** Bring sunscreen, sunglasses, and a hat to protect yourself from the sun's rays at higher elevations.
- **Tickets and Passes:** Purchase your Skyride tickets online in advance to save time and secure your spot.
- **Check Weather Conditions:** Mountain weather can change rapidly. Be prepared for varying conditions and check the weather forecast before heading up.

Getting There:

- **Skyride:** Take the Grouse Mountain Skyride from the base at 6400 Nancy Greene Way in North Vancouver.
- **Public Transit:** Accessible by public transit, take the SeaBus from downtown Vancouver to Lonsdale Quay, then take Bus 236 to Grouse Mountain.

A Mountain of Memories: Grouse Mountain is more than just a mountain; it's a gateway to nature's wonders, an invitation to conquer challenges, and a sanctuary for breathtaking moments. Whether you're seeking thrilling adventures on the slopes, tranquil strolls through alpine meadows, or a place to marvel at the beauty of British Columbia's wilderness, Grouse Mountain promises an unforgettable journey that will leave an indelible mark on your soul.

Granville Island

Nestled under the Granville Street Bridge in Vancouver, Granville Island beckons with its vibrant blend of artistic expression, delectable flavors, and a charming atmosphere that resonates with locals and visitors alike. A cultural enclave brimming with creativity, this urban haven invites you to dive into a world where artisans, merchants, and performers come together to create a symphony of sights, sounds, and tastes.

Address and GPS Position: Granville Island, Vancouver, BC V6H 3S3, Canada

GPS Coordinates: 49.269004, -123.133568

As you set foot on Granville Island, you'll be greeted by a lively energy that flows through its streets. Embark on a journey of discovery, where nooks and corners reveal unique treasures that capture the essence of the island's spirit.

A Feast for the Senses: *Public Market:* Begin your exploration at the Granville Island Public Market, a culinary wonderland where the aroma of freshly baked bread, vibrant displays of fruits, and artisanal cheeses tantalize your senses. Peruse stalls offering local seafood, gourmet chocolates, exotic spices, and a diverse array of international flavors.

Artisan Studios: Wander through Granville Island's artisan studios, where painters, potters, jewelers, and crafters showcase their talents. Engage with artists at work, witness the creative process, and perhaps take home a piece of their artistry.

Theatrical Delights: Catch a live performance at the Granville Island Theatre, where talented actors and performers bring stories to life in intimate settings.

Waterfront Wonders: *Granville Island Marina:* Stroll along the waterfront and marvel at the boats moored at the Granville Island

Marina. Feel the gentle sea breeze and soak in panoramic views of False Creek and downtown Vancouver.

Emily Carr University: Discover the prestigious Emily Carr University of Art + Design, a hub of creative education that contributes to the island's artistic ambiance.

Essential Tips and Information:

- **Operating Hours:** The Granville Island Public Market and many shops are open daily. Some businesses may have varying hours, so it's recommended to check in advance.
- **Parking:** Limited parking is available on the island. Consider using public transportation, walking, or biking to avoid parking challenges.
- **Shopping Bags:** Bring reusable shopping bags to carry your market finds and purchases.
- **Events and Festivals:** Check the island's event calendar for festivals, workshops, and performances that take place throughout the year.

Getting There:

- **Aquabus and False Creek Ferries:** Conveniently accessible by Aquabus or False Creek Ferries from various points along False Creek.
- **Granville Island Bus:** Take bus routes C21 or C23 from downtown Vancouver to Granville Island.

A Haven of Creativity and Delight: Granville Island isn't just a destination; it's an immersive experience that invites you to engage with art, indulge in culinary pleasures, and soak in the vibrant culture that defines Vancouver's artistic soul. Whether you're a connoisseur of the arts, a lover of gourmet cuisine, or simply seeking an escape from the ordinary, Granville Island promises to leave an indelible mark on your heart and memory.

Capilano Suspension Bridge Park

Located amidst the lush forests of North Vancouver, the Capilano Suspension Bridge Park stands as a gateway to an enchanting world of natural wonders and heart-pounding excitement. Spanning the Capilano River, this iconic suspension bridge and its surrounding attractions offer a thrilling blend of breathtaking views, rainforest exploration, and immersive experiences that awaken your sense of adventure.

Address and GPS Position: Capilano Suspension Bridge Park, 3735 Capilano Road, North Vancouver, BC V7R 4J1, Canada
   GPS Coordinates: 49.342974, -123.114972

As you step onto the historic Capilano Suspension Bridge, you'll be transported to a realm where the ancient rainforest canopy meets the river below. The bridge's gentle sway underfoot heightens your connection with nature, allowing you to witness the river's rush and the emerald foliage from a unique vantage point.

   Attractions and Adventures Await: *Treetops Adventure:* Embark on a journey through the forest canopy on the Treetops Adventure, a network of suspended walkways and platforms that allow you to explore the rainforest from high above the ground. As you stroll amidst the towering Douglas firs, experience the magic of the forest from a bird's-eye perspective.

Cliffwalk: For those seeking an adrenaline rush, the Cliffwalk offers an exhilarating experience. Walk along suspended walkways and cantilevered platforms that jut out from the granite cliffs, providing jaw-dropping views of the Capilano River.

Kids' Rainforest Explorer Program: Families with young adventurers can participate in the Kids' Rainforest Explorer Program, offering interactive and educational activities that highlight the park's natural beauty and biodiversity.

Tips for an Unforgettable Visit:

- **Operating Hours:** The park's operating hours vary by season. It's recommended to check the official website for current opening times.
- **Dress Comfortably:** Wear comfortable shoes suitable for walking and layers to adapt to changing weather conditions.
- **Photography:** Bring your camera to capture the stunning vistas and vibrant rainforest scenery.
- **Parking:** Limited on-site parking is available. Alternatively, consider taking public transit or using the park's shuttle service.

Getting There:

- **Public Transit:** Take bus routes 246, 247, or 236 from downtown Vancouver to Capilano Suspension Bridge Park.
- **Shuttle Service:** The park offers a convenient shuttle service from several locations in downtown Vancouver.

A Journey into Natural Splendor: The Capilano Suspension Bridge Park is more than an attraction; it's an immersive experience that connects you with the awe-inspiring beauty of British Columbia's rainforest. With its breathtaking vistas, heart-pounding adventures, and opportunities for reflection amidst nature's grandeur, the park invites you to forge a deeper connection with the world around you. As you traverse the bridge, walk the treetops, and marvel at the Cliffwalk, let the magic of the rainforest leave an indelible mark on your soul.

Lynn Canyon Park

Tucked away in North Vancouver, Lynn Canyon Park beckons with its pristine landscapes, lush forests, and captivating natural wonders. This hidden gem is a sanctuary of serenity, offering a serene escape from the bustling urban life. With its iconic suspension bridge, picturesque trails, and refreshing waters, Lynn Canyon Park invites you to immerse yourself in the embrace of nature.

Address and GPS Position: Lynn Canyon Park, 3690 Park Rd, North Vancouver, BC V7J 3G3, Canada
  GPS Coordinates: 49.3421° N, 123.0126° W

Step onto the historic Lynn Canyon Suspension Bridge, spanning the Lynn Creek below. As you traverse the swaying bridge, feel the connection with the lush forest and the soothing sounds of the creek echoing through the canyon. Gaze below at the clear emerald waters and boulders that create a picturesque scene.

  Trails and Explorations: *Twin Falls Bridge:* Embark on the Twin Falls Bridge trail, a moderate hike that leads you through towering trees and brings you to the breathtaking Twin Falls. The sight of cascading water amidst the verdant surroundings is a reward for your journey.

  Baden-Powell Trail: For those seeking a more challenging adventure, the Baden-Powell Trail offers a longer trek through the forest, connecting to other parks in the North Shore.

Swimming and Cooling Off: *Lynn Creek Pools:* On warm days, seek refuge in the cool waters of Lynn Creek Pools, natural pools formed by the creek's flow. Dip your toes in the refreshing water or take a leisurely swim amidst nature's beauty.

Essential Tips and Information:

- **Park Hours:** Lynn Canyon Park is open year-round, and the hours vary by season. Plan your visit accordingly.
- **Dress Appropriately:** Wear comfortable walking shoes suitable for trails, and bring a light jacket as the weather can change quickly.
- **Photography:** Don't forget your camera to capture the stunning landscapes and natural beauty.
- **Leave No Trace:** Respect the environment by packing out what you bring and keeping the park clean.

Getting There:

- **Public Transit:** Take bus route 227 from Lonsdale Quay in North Vancouver to Lynn Canyon Park.
- **Driving:** From Vancouver, follow Trans-Canada Hwy/BC-1 W and exit onto Lynn Valley Rd. Continue on Lynn Valley Rd and follow the signs to Lynn Canyon Park.

Lynn Canyon Park offers more than just a nature retreat; it provides a gateway to a realm where the gentle whispers of the forest, the tranquil embrace of the creek, and the rustling leaves create a symphony of calm. Whether you're crossing the suspension bridge, exploring the trails, or simply finding solace by the water's edge, Lynn Canyon Park promises a rejuvenating experience that will stay with you long after you've left its embrace.

Pacific Spirit Regional Park

Located within the vibrant city of Vancouver, Pacific Spirit Regional Park stands as an oasis of pristine wilderness and natural beauty. This expansive parkland, characterized by lush forests, meandering trails, and diverse ecosystems, invites you to embark on a journey of discovery and serenity.

Address and GPS Position: Pacific Spirit Regional Park, Vancouver, BC V6T 1Z3, Canada
   GPS Coordinates: 49.266136, -123.217226

As you step into Pacific Spirit Regional Park, a sense of tranquility washes over you. The park's extensive network of trails winds through towering trees, revealing pockets of old-growth forest, vibrant meadows, and delicate wetlands. Each step offers a new perspective on the natural world, and the symphony of birdsong envelops you in a soothing embrace.

Exploring the Trails: *Salish Trail:* Follow the Salish Trail, a wheelchair-accessible path that provides a gentle introduction to the park's beauty. Along the way, you'll encounter informative signs that offer insights into the area's rich biodiversity.

South Campus Trail: For a longer journey, explore the South Campus Trail, which winds through diverse habitats, including towering conifers and flourishing understory vegetation.

Wildlife and Botanical Delights: *Wildlife Viewing:* Keep an eye out for the park's resident wildlife, including deer, owls, and various bird species. The park's quietude creates a haven for these creatures, offering visitors a chance to observe them in their natural habitat.

Botanical Garden: Discover the Nitobe Memorial Garden, a serene Japanese garden within the park that features meticulously designed landscapes, teahouses, and serene ponds.

Tips and Essentials:

- **Park Hours:** Pacific Spirit Regional Park is open year-round from dawn to dusk.
- **Footwear:** Wear comfortable hiking shoes suitable for trails and changing terrain.
- **Weather Preparedness:** Bring weather-appropriate clothing and layers, as weather conditions can vary.
- **Photography:** Capture the park's beauty and diverse ecosystems through your camera lens.

Getting There:

- **Public Transit:** Take public transit to the University of British Columbia (UBC) campus and access the park from various trailheads.
- **Driving:** From Vancouver, follow W 4th Ave westbound, which leads you to the park's western edge.

Pacific Spirit Regional Park is not merely a park; it's a sanctuary where you can step away from the urban hustle and immerse yourself in the serenity of nature. Whether you're seeking a contemplative stroll, a refreshing hike, or a moment of connection with the wilderness, the park's diverse landscapes and peaceful atmosphere offer a space to rejuvenate and connect with the world around you.

Garibaldi Provincial Park

Found in the Coast Mountain Range of British Columbia, Garibaldi Provincial Park unfolds as a breathtaking tapestry of alpine meadows, glacial lakes, and rugged landscapes. This wilderness sanctuary beckons adventurers to explore its diverse trails, witness its stunning vistas, and immerse themselves in the awe-inspiring beauty of its backcountry terrain.

Address and GPS Position: Garibaldi Provincial Park, Squamish-Lillooet D, BC, Canada
   GPS Coordinates: 49.9689° N, 123.0132° W

From the moment you set foot in Garibaldi Provincial Park, the grandeur of nature envelops you. Towering peaks, turquoise lakes, and fields of wildflowers create a surreal backdrop that captivates the senses and ignites the spirit of adventure.

   Trails and Hiking Adventures: *Garibaldi Lake Trail:* Embark on the iconic Garibaldi Lake Trail, a moderate hike that leads you through dense forests, alpine meadows, and culminates at the serene and glacier-fed Garibaldi Lake. The views of the lake, surrounded by snowy peaks, are nothing short of breathtaking.

   Black Tusk Trail: For more experienced hikers, the Black Tusk Trail offers a challenging trek that rewards you with panoramic views from the summit of the Black Tusk volcanic pinnacle.

   Camping and Backcountry Exploration: *Backcountry Camping:* Immerse yourself in the park's wilderness by camping in its backcountry sites. Enjoy a night under the stars, surrounded by the tranquil sounds of nature.

Essential Tips and Information:

- **Camping Permits:** If planning to camp overnight, obtain a camping permit in advance from BC Parks.
- **Bear Safety:** Be aware of bear safety measures, including proper food storage and carrying bear spray.
- **Leave No Trace:** Respect the environment by packing out what you bring and leaving the park pristine.
- **Weather Preparedness:** Weather conditions in the alpine can change rapidly, so be prepared for varying conditions.

Getting There:

- **Driving:** From Vancouver, take the Sea-to-Sky Highway (Highway 99) to Squamish. Follow the signs to the park's various trailheads, such as the Diamond Head Trailhead.

A Wilderness Wonderland Awaits: Garibaldi Provincial Park is more than a park; it's an invitation to embark on a journey into the heart of nature's majesty. Whether you're marveling at the alpine landscapes, conquering challenging trails, or simply finding solace in the serenity of the backcountry, the park offers an escape from the ordinary and a chance to connect with the extraordinary beauty of the natural world. As you traverse its trails and gaze upon its pristine lakes, let Garibaldi Provincial Park etch its indelible mark on your memory and spirit.

Cypress Provincial Park

Nestled in the North Shore Mountains near Vancouver, Cypress Provincial Park unveils a world of alpine beauty, year-round recreation, and breathtaking vistas. This mountainous sanctuary invites outdoor enthusiasts to embrace its trails, ski slopes, and serene landscapes, offering an escape into the embrace of nature's grandeur.

Address and GPS Position: Cypress Provincial Park, Cypress Bowl Rd, West Vancouver, BC V7V 3N9, Canada
  GPS Coordinates: 49.3978° N, 123.1985° W

As you enter Cypress Provincial Park, you're greeted by towering trees, pristine meadows, and stunning mountain views. Whether it's the tranquil stillness of winter or the vibrant bloom of summer, the park's allure is ever-present.

Skiing and Snowsports: *Downhill Skiing and Snowboarding:* In the winter months, Cypress Mountain transforms into a playground for skiers and snowboarders, with slopes catering to all skill levels. The breathtaking views of the surrounding landscape from the slopes add to the experience.

Cross-Country Skiing: Embrace the tranquility of cross-country skiing as you glide through snow-covered trails, surrounded by the hush of the winter forest.

Summer Hiking and Exploration: *Yew Lake Trail:* Embark on the Yew Lake Trail, a gentle loop that meanders through lush forests and leads you to the tranquil Yew Lake, reflecting the surrounding mountains.

Essential Tips and Information:

- **Operating Hours:** The park's operating hours vary by season and activity. Be sure to check the official website for the most up-to-date information.
- **Weather Preparedness:** Weather conditions can change rapidly in the mountains. Dress in layers and bring essentials like sunscreen and water.

- **Parking:** Limited parking is available at the park. Consider carpooling or using shuttle services during peak times.

Getting There:

- **Driving:** From Vancouver, follow Highway 1 (Trans-Canada Highway) westbound. Take exit 8 for Cypress Bowl Road and follow signs to the park.

Cypress Provincial Park is more than a destination; it's a celebration of alpine splendor and outdoor vitality. Whether you're carving down the slopes in winter, embracing the trails in summer, or simply basking in the panoramic views that stretch before you, the park offers an escape from the ordinary and a chance to revel in the extraordinary beauty of the natural world. As you immerse yourself in its landscapes and take in the sweeping vistas, let Cypress Provincial Park etch its indelible mark on your memory and leave you with a renewed appreciation for the majesty of the mountains.

Queen Elizabeth Park

Nestled within the heart of Vancouver, Queen Elizabeth Park unfolds as a horticultural masterpiece and a haven of natural beauty. With its meticulously designed gardens, panoramic vistas, and a myriad of recreational opportunities, this urban oasis invites visitors to escape the urban hustle and immerse themselves in a world of tranquility and splendor.

Address and GPS Position: Queen Elizabeth Park, 4600 Cambie St,

Vancouver, BC V5Y 2M4, Canada
GPS Coordinates: 49.2415° N, 123.1116° W

From the moment you enter Queen Elizabeth Park, a symphony of colors, scents, and textures envelops you. The park's gardens are a testament to horticultural artistry, showcasing a diverse collection of plants from around the world.

Seasonal Highlights: *Sunken Garden:* Descend into the enchanting Sunken Garden, where vibrant flower beds, tranquil pools, and cascading waterfalls create a visual masterpiece that changes with the seasons.

Rose Garden: Bask in the beauty of the Rose Garden, a fragrant oasis boasting an array of rose varieties in bloom during the warmer months.

Arboretum: Stroll through the Arboretum and discover an impressive collection of trees, showcasing a tapestry of foliage colors during the fall months.

Panoramic Views and Recreation: *Queen Elizabeth Park Lookout:* Ascend to the Queen Elizabeth Park Lookout, the highest point in Vancouver. From here, you're treated to panoramic vistas of the city skyline, surrounding mountains, and beyond.

Tennis Courts and Lawn Bowling: Engage in recreational activities by utilizing the park's tennis courts or trying your hand at lawn bowling.

Tips and Essentials:

- **Park Hours:** Queen Elizabeth Park is open year-round from dawn to dusk.
- **Photography:** Bring your camera to capture the vibrant gardens and breathtaking views.
- **Footwear:** Wear comfortable shoes suitable for walking, as the park covers a considerable area.

Getting There:

- **Public Transit:** Take the Canada Line SkyTrain to King Edward Station, and the park is within walking distance.
- **Driving:** From downtown Vancouver, follow Cambie Street southbound until you reach the park.

Queen Elizabeth Park is a sanctuary where you can escape the urban buzz and immerse yourself in the serenity of nature's beauty. Whether you're strolling amidst the meticulously manicured gardens, gazing at the city from the lookout, or simply finding solace in the peaceful surroundings, the park offers a space to rejuvenate and connect with the world's natural wonders. As you explore its gardens and absorb its panoramic views, let Queen Elizabeth Park etch its indelible mark on your memory and spirit.

Kitsilano Beach (Kits Beach)

Seated at the edge of Vancouver's Kitsilano neighborhood, Kitsilano Beach, affectionately known as "Kits Beach," exudes a laid-back coastal vibe that perfectly encapsulates the spirit of the city. With its sun-soaked shores, stunning views, and vibrant atmosphere, Kits Beach offers a slice of beachfront paradise right in the heart of the city.

Address and GPS Position: Kitsilano Beach (Kits Beach), 1499 Arbutus St, Vancouver, BC V6J 5N2, Canada
   GPS Coordinates: 49.2712° N, 123.1540° W

As you step onto the sandy shores of Kits Beach, you're greeted by the soothing rhythm of waves and a panoramic view that stretches across the waters of English Bay. The beach's golden sands and expansive waterfront invite you to unwind, bask in the sun, and embrace the coastal charm.

Activities and Amenities: *Swimming and Sunbathing:* Take a refreshing dip in the waters of English Bay or lounge on the beach with a good book. The gentle waves and laid-back atmosphere make it a prime spot for relaxation.

Volleyball Courts: Engage in a friendly game of beach volleyball with friends or join a pickup match on the sandy courts.

Seawall Stroll and Biking: Explore the scenic Vancouver Seawall that passes through Kits Beach, offering a picturesque pathway for walking, jogging, or biking along the waterfront.

Water Sports and Recreation: *Stand-Up Paddleboarding (SUP):* Rent a paddleboard and glide across the calm waters, enjoying a unique perspective of the shoreline.

Kayaking: Embark on a kayaking adventure and explore English Bay's coastline from the water, taking in views of the city and the North Shore Mountains.

Beachside Cafés and Dining: *Local Eateries:* Adjacent to Kits Beach, you'll find a variety of cafés, bistros, and eateries offering everything from casual beachside fare to gourmet meals with ocean views.

Tips and Essentials:

- **Beach Hours:** Kits Beach is open year-round, but swimming conditions and water temperatures vary by season.
- **Parking:** Limited pay parking is available nearby, but the beach is also accessible by public transit and bike lanes.
- **Sun Protection:** Bring sunscreen, a hat, and sunglasses to stay comfortable under the sun.

Getting There:

- **Public Transit:** Take bus routes 2, 22, or 32 from downtown Vancouver to Kitsilano Beach.
- **Driving:** From downtown, head west on Cornwall Avenue, which leads you directly to Kits Beach.

Kitsilano Beach is a celebration of coastal living and urban cool. Whether you're lounging on the sand, engaging in water sports, or simply soaking in the vibrant atmosphere, the beach offers a quintessential Vancouver experience. As you enjoy the views of English Bay and revel in the beachside charm, let Kitsilano Beach etch its indelible mark on your memories and leave you with a sun-kissed smile that lingers long after you've left its shores.

English Bay Beach

Located along the vibrant West End of Vancouver, English Bay Beach presents an idyllic oasis where sandy shores, sparkling waters, and breathtaking sunsets converge. This iconic urban beach is a gathering place for locals and visitors alike, offering a front-row seat to nature's beauty and a slice of coastal paradise.

Address and GPS Position: English Bay Beach, 1799 Beach Ave, Vancouver, BC V6G 1Y9, Canada

GPS Coordinates: 49.2894° N, 123.1407° W

As you step onto English Bay Beach, the expansive stretch of sandy shoreline invites you to kick off your shoes and embrace the carefree ambiance. Whether you're seeking relaxation, active pursuits, or simply a serene spot to soak in the scenery, the beach offers a canvas of possibilities.

Sunsets and Views: Sunsets at English Bay Beach are legendary. As the sun dips below the horizon, the sky comes alive with a vibrant palette of colors, painting a picture that's both breathtaking and awe-inspiring. Find a cozy spot on the sand, a waterfront bench, or the grassy knolls nearby to witness this natural spectacle.

Activities and Amenities: *Swimming and Sunbathing:* The calm waters of English Bay are ideal for a refreshing swim or lounging under the sun. The gentle waves and inviting ambiance make it a favorite spot for sunbathers.

Seawall Promenade: Take a leisurely stroll or bike ride along the iconic Vancouver Seawall that passes by English Bay Beach. The scenic pathway offers stunning views of the coastline and downtown Vancouver.

Beachside Cafés and Dining: *Local Eateries:* Adjacent to the beach, you'll find charming beachside cafés and restaurants offering a variety of cuisine, from fresh seafood to international fare.

Tips and Essentials:

- **Beach Hours:** English Bay Beach is open year-round, and its beauty varies by season. Check sunset times for the best sunset-viewing experience.
- **Parking:** Limited pay parking is available nearby, but the beach is accessible by public transit and bike lanes.
- **Sun Protection:** Bring sunscreen, sunglasses, and a beach towel or blanket for maximum comfort.

Getting There:

- **Public Transit:** Take bus routes 5, 6, or C23 from downtown

Vancouver to English Bay Beach.
- **Driving:** From downtown, head west on Davie Street or Beach Avenue, both of which lead you to English Bay Beach.

English Bay Beach is a front-row seat to Vancouver's coastal allure and natural wonders. Whether you're gazing at the sunset's mesmerizing hues, playing in the waves, or simply savoring the beachside atmosphere, the beach offers a sensory experience that captures the essence of the city. As you soak in the views, feel the sand beneath your feet, and revel in the coastal charm, let English Bay Beach etch its indelible mark on your memories and leave you with a sense of tranquility and wonder that lingers long after the sun has set.

Granville Island

Nestled in the heart of Vancouver, Granville Island is a captivating enclave that fuses creativity, culture, and culinary delights into a vibrant tapestry. This urban treasure trove invites you to explore artisan studios, indulge in gourmet pleasures, and immerse yourself in a world where artistic expression flourishes at every turn.

Address and GPS Position: Granville Island, Vancouver, BC V6H 3S3, Canada
GPS Coordinates: 49.269004, -123.133568
An Artistic Playground: As you step onto Granville Island, a palpable energy envelops you. The island's historic industrial buildings have been transformed into a playground for artisans, craftsmen, and performers, creating a living canvas of creative expression.
Exploring the Public Market: *Granville Island Public Market:* Begin your exploration at the Granville Island Public Market, a bustling

emporium where the scents of freshly baked goods, colorful produce, and gourmet treats tantalize the senses. Discover a cornucopia of local and international flavors, from artisan cheeses to exotic spices.

Artisan Studios and Galleries: *Art Studios:* Wander through the island's artisan studios, where painters, sculptors, jewelers, and craftsmen work their magic. Witness the creative process, engage with artists, and perhaps take home a one-of-a-kind masterpiece.

Cultural Experiences and Entertainment: *Granville Island Theatre:* Catch a live performance at the Granville Island Theatre, where talented actors and musicians bring stories to life in intimate settings.

Outdoor Performances: Throughout the island, street performers captivate audiences with their talents, adding to the island's vibrant atmosphere.

Waterfront Delights: *Granville Island Marina:* Stroll along the waterfront and admire the boats moored at the Granville Island Marina. Breathe in the sea breeze and enjoy panoramic views of False Creek and the city skyline.

Essential Tips and Information:

- **Operating Hours:** The Granville Island Public Market and many shops are open daily. Some businesses may have varying hours, so it's recommended to check in advance.
- **Parking:** Limited parking is available on the island. Consider using public transportation, walking, or biking to avoid parking challenges.
- **Cash and Cards:** While most places accept credit cards, it's a good idea to carry some cash for smaller vendors.

Getting There:

- **Aquabus and False Creek Ferries:** Conveniently accessible by Aquabus or False Creek Ferries from various points along False Creek.
- **Granville Island Bus:** Take bus routes C21 or C23 from downtown Vancouver to Granville Island.

Granville Island isn't just a destination; it's a celebration of artistic ingenuity, culinary exploration, and cultural diversity. Whether you're discovering the hidden treasures of the public market, witnessing artists at work, or simply absorbing the island's vibrant ambiance, Granville Island promises a sensory journey that leaves an indelible mark on your heart and memory. As you explore its nooks and corners, taste its flavors, and engage with its creative spirits, let Granville Island inspire your imagination and enrich your connection with Vancouver's cultural mosaic.

Gastown

Nestled in the heart of downtown Vancouver, Gastown stands as a testament to the city's rich history, artistic spirit, and vibrant urban culture. This iconic neighborhood, known for its cobblestone streets, historic buildings, and artistic flair, invites you to explore its charming streets, discover hidden gems, and immerse yourself in the fusion of old-world elegance and modern vibrancy.

Address and GPS Position: Gastown, Vancouver, BC, Canada
  GPS Coordinates: 49.2830° N, 123.1062° W

As you wander through Gastown's cobbled streets, you'll be transported to an era gone by. The neighborhood's well-preserved architecture, vintage lampposts, and atmospheric alleyways evoke a sense of nostalgia and intrigue.

Gastown's Iconic Attractions: *Gastown Steam Clock:* Witness the charm of the Gastown Steam Clock, an iconic landmark that billows steam and plays chimes to the delight of passersby.

Gassy Jack Statue: Pay homage to John "Gassy Jack" Deighton, the colorful character who founded the area in 1867, by visiting the Gassy Jack statue located in Maple Tree Square.

Artistic Expression and Galleries: *Art Galleries:* Explore art galleries and studios that dot the neighborhood, showcasing a diverse array of artistic expression, from contemporary to traditional.

Shopping and Boutiques: *Local Boutiques:* Peruse the boutique shops that line Gastown's streets, offering everything from handcrafted goods and vintage finds to cutting-edge fashion and unique accessories.

Dining and Culinary Delights: *Gastown's Dining Scene:* Experience Gastown's culinary scene, which blends creativity with local flavors. From gourmet restaurants to charming cafés, the neighborhood offers a range of dining options.

Nightlife and Entertainment: *Gastown After Dark:* As the sun sets, Gastown transforms into a hub of nightlife and entertainment. Discover live music venues, cocktail lounges, and pubs that pulse with energy.

Essential Tips and Information:

- **Walking Shoes:** Wear comfortable walking shoes, as Gastown's cobblestone streets and charming alleys are best explored on foot.
- **Public Transportation:** Gastown is accessible by public transit and is a short walk from the Waterfront SkyTrain station.
- **Time to Visit:** The neighborhood is lively throughout the day, but evenings offer a special atmosphere with illuminated streets and bustling nightlife.

Getting There:

- **SkyTrain:** Take the SkyTrain to Waterfront Station, and Gastown is just a short walk away.
- **Driving:** If driving, use the address of a nearby landmark or parking garage, as Gastown's streets are primarily pedestrian-friendly.

Gastown is a journey through time, a canvas of creativity, and a living testament to Vancouver's spirit. Whether you're captivated by the steam clock's chimes, savoring culinary delights, or simply strolling through its streets, Gastown invites you to be a part of its narrative. As you immerse yourself in its charm, let Gastown's fusion of history and modernity inspire you and leave you with a lasting appreciation for the dynamic energy that defines this cultural hub.

Chinatown

Easily found in the heart of Vancouver, Chinatown stands as a living testament to the city's diverse cultural landscape and historical heritage. This vibrant neighborhood, with its intricate architecture, bustling markets, and cultural landmarks, invites you to explore its alleys, savor its flavors, and immerse yourself in the tapestry of Chinese culture that unfolds at every turn.

Address and GPS Position: Chinatown, Vancouver, BC, Canada
GPS Coordinates: 49.2795° N, 123.1012° W

As you step into Chinatown, you're transported to a world where East meets West, tradition meets innovation, and the past intertwines with the present. The neighborhood's rich history and cultural significance are palpable in its every corner.

Exploring Cultural Landmarks: *Dr. Sun Yat-sen Classical Chinese Garden:* Discover the tranquility of the Dr. Sun Yat-sen Classical Chinese Garden, a masterpiece that embodies the principles of Chinese garden design and provides a haven of serenity.**(More about this later)**

Historic Charm and Architecture: *Heritage Buildings:* Marvel at the neighborhood's historic architecture, with ornate façades, vibrant murals, and intricately adorned buildings that tell the story of Chinatown's evolution.

Culinary Delights and Markets: *Chinatown Night Market:* During the summer months, explore the vibrant Chinatown Night Market, where stalls come alive with an array of food, crafts, and entertainment.

Shopping and Boutiques: *Local Shops:* Peruse the shops and boutiques that offer a diverse range of goods, from traditional herbs and teas to contemporary fashion and artisanal crafts.

Cultural Diversity and Events: *Chinese New Year Celebrations:* Join in the festivities during Chinese New Year, when Chinatown comes alive with dragon dances, lantern displays, and cultural performances.

Essential Tips and Information:

- **Footwear:** Wear comfortable walking shoes to explore the neighborhood's alleys and streets.
- **Public Transportation:** Chinatown is accessible by public transit, with several bus routes and SkyTrain stations nearby.
- **Cash and Cards:** While most places accept credit cards, having some cash on hand is useful for smaller vendors.

Getting There:

- **SkyTrain and Bus:** Take the SkyTrain to Stadium-Chinatown Station or Main Street-Science World Station, both of which are within walking distance of Chinatown.

Chinatown is a living embodiment of history, cultural identity, and community resilience. Whether you're exploring its intricate gardens, savoring traditional cuisine, or simply absorbing the atmosphere of its streets, Chinatown invites you to embrace the beauty of diversity and the richness of its heritage. As you navigate its alleys, taste its flavors, and engage with its traditions, let Chinatown's vibrant spirit inspire your sense of wonder and leave you with a lasting connection to Vancouver's cultural mosaic.

Commercial Drive

Nestled in East Vancouver, Commercial Drive, often referred to simply as "The Drive," radiates an authentic and eclectic spirit that encapsulates the city's cultural diversity and artistic expression. This vibrant neighborhood, with its diverse array of shops, eateries, and cultural spaces, invites you to embrace its laid-back charm, celebrate its community, and immerse yourself in a tapestry of urban vibrancy.
   Address and GPS Position: Commercial Drive, Vancouver, BC, Canada
   GPS Coordinates: 49.2718° N, 123.0699° W

As you step onto Commercial Drive, you'll feel the beat of the neighborhood's bohemian heart. The area's colorful murals, quirky shops, and lively atmosphere set the stage for a unique and immersive experience.
   Exploring Cultural Treasures: *Little Italy Vibes:* Immerse yourself in the Italian charm of the neighborhood, with European-style cafes,

pizzerias, and gelato shops that offer a slice of Mediterranean delight.

Diverse Dining and Cuisine: *Ethnic Eateries:* Embark on a culinary journey with a plethora of international restaurants representing cuisines from around the world. From Vietnamese pho to Ethiopian injera, The Drive is a food lover's paradise.

Artistic Expression and Boutiques: *Local Boutiques:* Stroll through the neighborhood's boutiques, vintage shops, and independent stores, where you can find unique clothing, artisanal crafts, and quirky finds.

Cafés and Community Spaces: *Coffee Culture:* Embrace the café culture of Commercial Drive, where you can find cozy spots to sip on coffee, people-watch, and connect with locals.

Entertainment and Events: *Live Music and Venues:* Explore the live music scene with various venues hosting performances, from indie bands to jazz ensembles.

Essential Tips and Information:

- **Walking:** Wear comfortable shoes suitable for walking, as The Drive is best explored on foot.
- **Public Transportation:** The neighborhood is accessible by several bus routes, making it convenient to travel to and from the area.
- **Parking:** Limited street parking is available, so consider using public transportation or alternative modes of transport.

Getting There:

- **Bus:** Take bus routes 20, 22, or 9 from downtown Vancouver to Commercial Drive.

A Bohemian Gem of Creativity and Community: Commercial Drive is an embodiment of East Vancouver's free-spirited identity, artistic energy, and cultural fusion. Whether you're savoring international flavors, perusing eclectic shops, or simply absorbing the neighborhood's lively vibe, The Drive invites you to be a part of its dynamic narrative. As you explore its nooks and corners, engage with its local characters, and celebrate its diversity, let Commercial Drive inspire your sense of curiosity and connection to the heart of Vancouver's creative spirit.

UBC Museum of Anthropology

Located within the captivating campus of the University of British Columbia, the UBC Museum of Anthropology (MOA) is a cultural treasure that showcases the rich tapestry of Indigenous cultures from across Canada and around the world. This immersive institution invites visitors to explore breathtaking art, artifacts, and narratives that celebrate human creativity, tradition, and the power of cultural expression.

Address and GPS Position: UBC Museum of Anthropology, 6393 NW Marine Dr, Vancouver, BC V6T 1Z2, Canada
  GPS Coordinates: 49.269944, -123.259663

Upon entering the MOA, you're greeted by towering totem poles, which are a symbol of the museum's commitment to preserving and sharing Indigenous heritage. The museum's architecture, designed by Arthur Erickson, is a masterpiece in itself, seamlessly integrating with its natural surroundings.
  Exhibits and Collections: *Indigenous Art and Artifacts:* The MOA boasts an impressive collection of Indigenous art, showcasing intricate carvings, masks, textiles, and other artistic expressions that reflect the

cultural diversity and heritage of Indigenous communities.

Multicultural Heritage: Beyond Indigenous cultures, the museum's exhibits span the globe, offering insights into various cultures and traditions from Asia, Oceania, Africa, and the Americas.

Great Hall and Totem Poles: *The Great Hall:* Immerse yourself in the awe-inspiring Great Hall, surrounded by totem poles and sculptures that stand as guardians of cultural narratives and history.

Cultural Events and Programming: *Public Programs:* The MOA offers a range of programs, workshops, and lectures that delve deeper into the exhibits and provide opportunities for engagement and learning.

Essential Tips and Information:

- **Operating Hours:** Check the official website for the most up-to-date operating hours and exhibition details.
- **Admission:** Admission fees apply, with discounts for students, seniors, and children.
- **Guided Tours:** Consider joining a guided tour to gain deeper insights into the exhibits and the stories they hold.

Getting There:

- **Public Transit:** Take public transit to UBC, and the museum is a short walk from the main bus loop.
- **Driving:** From downtown Vancouver, follow West 4th Avenue westbound, which leads to the UBC campus.

The UBC Museum of Anthropology is a portal to a world of cultural diversity, heritage, and human connection. Whether you're marveling at intricate carvings, exploring the Great Hall, or engaging in the museum's educational programs, the MOA offers a profound journey into the heart of human creativity and resilience. As you explore its exhibits and immerse yourself in its narratives, let the UBC Museum of Anthropology inspire your appreciation for the interconnectedness of cultures and the power of storytelling.

Vancouver Art Gallery

Located in the heart of downtown Vancouver, the Vancouver Art Gallery stands as a beacon of artistic expression, a repository of cultural heritage, and a space that celebrates the power of visual arts to inspire, provoke, and unite. With its diverse collection, thought-provoking exhibitions, and commitment to fostering creativity, the gallery offers an immersive journey into the world of art.

Address and GPS Position: Vancouver Art Gallery, 750 Hornby St, Vancouver, BC V6Z 2H7, Canada

GPS Coordinates: 49.2820° N, 123.1208° W

From the moment you enter the Vancouver Art Gallery, you're transported into a realm of creativity and imagination. The gallery's spacious and elegant setting provides an ideal backdrop for exploring a wide range of artistic styles, periods, and genres.

Permanent Collections and Exhibitions: *Group of Seven and Canadian Art:* Immerse yourself in the works of iconic Canadian artists like the Group of Seven, whose landscapes celebrate the country's natural beauty.

International and Contemporary Art: The gallery also houses an impressive collection of international and contemporary art, offering insights into diverse cultural perspectives.

Rotating Exhibitions and Events: *Temporary Exhibitions:* The gallery hosts rotating exhibitions that feature works from around the world, exploring themes that range from historical to contemporary.

Special Events: Check the gallery's calendar for special events, talks, and workshops that provide deeper insights into the artworks and artistic processes.

Emily Carr Collection: *Emily Carr:* The Vancouver Art Gallery holds a significant collection of works by Canadian artist Emily Carr, allowing visitors to explore her iconic depictions of the West Coast landscape.

Essential Tips and Information:

- **Operating Hours:** Check the official website for current opening hours, exhibition details, and admission fees.
- **Admission:** Admission rates vary, with discounts available for students, seniors, and children.
- **Guided Tours:** Consider joining a guided tour to enhance your understanding of the artworks and their historical context.

Getting There:

- **Public Transit:** The gallery is easily accessible by public transit, with nearby bus stops and SkyTrain stations.
- **Driving:** Parking is available nearby, and the gallery's central location makes it convenient to reach by car.

Whether you're admiring iconic Canadian works, engaging with contemporary art, or attending an enlightening event, the gallery offers an opportunity to connect with the world's visual heritage. As you wander through its halls, contemplate its exhibits, and appreciate the breadth of human imagination, let the Vancouver Art Gallery leave an indelible mark on your artistic spirit and deepen your appreciation for the transformative power of art.

Vancouver Public Library

Nestled in the heart of downtown Vancouver, the Vancouver Public Library (VPL) is more than just a repository of books; it's a cultural landmark that fosters learning, creativity, and community engagement. With its iconic architecture, diverse collections, and wide range of services, the library stands as a hub where knowledge thrives and the spirit of discovery comes alive.

Central Branch Address and GPS Position: Vancouver Public Library - Central Branch, 350 W Georgia St, Vancouver, BC V6B 6B1, Canada

GPS Coordinates: 49.2790° N, 123.1152° W

Designed by architect Moshe Safdie, the Central Branch of the VPL is an architectural masterpiece that captivates visitors with its iconic design. The library's stunning glass and steel structure serves as an inviting space where literature and imagination converge.

Collections and Resources: *Vast Collections:* The VPL boasts a vast collection of books, magazines, digital resources, and multimedia materials that cater to readers of all ages and interests.

Multilingual Offerings: Explore the library's diverse offerings, including literature in multiple languages, reflecting the city's multicultural fabric.

Spaces for Learning and Creativity: *Reading Areas:* Find quiet reading areas, study spaces, and comfortable seating where you can immerse yourself in the world of literature.

Innovation Hub: The library offers an Innovation Hub equipped with technology for creativity, digital media production, and experimentation.

Special Programs and Events: *Author Talks and Workshops:* The library hosts an array of events, including author talks, workshops, book clubs, and discussions on various topics.

Essential Tips and Information:

- **Operating Hours:** Check the official website for the current operating hours, event schedule, and service details.
- **Library Card:** You can obtain a free library card to borrow materials, access digital resources, and take advantage of the library's services.
- **Wi-Fi and Computers:** The library provides free Wi-Fi and computer access for visitors.

Getting There:

- **Public Transit:** The library is conveniently located near public transit routes, including SkyTrain stations and bus stops.
- **Driving:** If driving, consider using nearby parking facilities or metered street parking.

The Vancouver Public Library isn't just a library; it's a sanctuary for book lovers, a catalyst for learning, and a dynamic community space. Whether you're exploring the bookshelves, attending an author talk, or simply finding solace in its quiet corners, the library offers an invitation to connect with knowledge, culture, and the city's vibrant spirit. As you delve into its pages, attend its events, and bask in its architectural beauty, let the Vancouver Public Library enrich your mind, ignite your curiosity, and remind you of the transformative power of literature and shared ideas.

Vancouver Lookout

Perched high above the bustling streets of downtown Vancouver, the Vancouver Lookout offers an unparalleled vantage point to admire the city's skyline, natural beauty, and vibrant urban tapestry. This iconic observation deck invites visitors to ascend to new heights and immerse themselves in panoramic vistas that showcase the city's breathtaking landscapes and dynamic energy.

Address and GPS Position: Vancouver Lookout, 555 W Hastings St, Vancouver, BC V6B 4N6, Canada
  GPS Coordinates: 49.2852° N, 123.1129° W

As you step into the Vancouver Lookout, an elevator whisks you high above the city streets, transporting you to an observation deck that opens up to a 360-degree view of Vancouver's stunning surroundings.

Unparalleled City Views: From the Lookout's elevated perch, you can gaze upon landmarks such as the stunning Stanley Park, the vibrant Granville Island, and the waters of English Bay and Burrard Inlet that frame the city.

Natural Beauty and Urban Splendor: Beyond the city, your view extends to the majestic North Shore Mountains, creating a captivating contrast between the urban landscape and the rugged natural beauty that surrounds Vancouver.

Time to Take it All In: Day or night, the Vancouver Lookout offers a unique experience. Witness the city as it awakens to the morning sun or basks in the twinkling lights of the evening.

Interactive Displays and Information: The observation deck features informative displays that highlight key landmarks and neighborhoods visible from the Lookout, providing context to the city's layout and history.

Essential Tips and Information:

- **Operating Hours:** Check the official website for current operating hours and admission fees.
- **Photography:** Bring your camera or smartphone to capture the sweeping views from the observation deck.
- **Weather Considerations:** Weather conditions can impact visibility, so choose a clear day for the best viewing experience.

Getting There:

- **Public Transit:** The Vancouver Lookout is conveniently located near public transit routes, including SkyTrain stations and bus stops.
- **Driving:** If driving, there are parking facilities nearby, and the Lookout is centrally located.

Whether you're admiring the cityscape, tracing the coastline, or marveling at the convergence of nature and urban life, the Lookout offers an opportunity to connect with Vancouver's essence from the sky. As you take in the views, contemplate the city's ever-changing landscape, and feel the pulse of the metropolis beneath you, let the Vancouver Lookout etch an unforgettable panorama into your memory and deepen your connection to this vibrant city.

VanDusen Botanical Garden

Nestled in the heart of Vancouver, the VanDusen Botanical Garden is a living testament to the wonders of nature's artistry and the diversity of plant life from around the world. With its meticulously curated gardens, serene pathways, and immersive horticultural experiences, this enchanting oasis invites visitors to escape into a world of tranquility, exploration, and botanical marvels.

Address and GPS Position: VanDusen Botanical Garden, 5251 Oak St, Vancouver, BC V6M 4H1, Canada
GPS Coordinates: 49.2387° N, 123.1283° W

As you enter the VanDusen Botanical Garden, you'll be greeted by a symphony of colors, fragrances, and textures that showcase the beauty and diversity of plant life from across the globe.

Meticulously Curated Gardens: *Elizabethan Maze:* Embark on a playful journey through the Elizabethan Maze, a labyrinth that beckons exploration and adventure.

Sino-Himalayan Garden: Immerse yourself in the tranquility of the Sino-Himalayan Garden, which showcases plants from the diverse ecosystems of the Himalayas.

Blooms and Seasonal Delights: *Floral Spectacles:* Throughout the year, the garden showcases a variety of seasonal blooms, from vibrant spring blossoms to fall foliage.

Visitor-Friendly Amenities: *Visitor Centre:* Begin your visit at the Visitor Centre, where you can gather information, obtain maps, and learn about upcoming events.

Garden Shop: Explore the Garden Shop, which offers a range of botanical gifts, books, and souvenirs inspired by the garden's natural beauty.

Family-Friendly Activities: *Children's Garden:* The whimsical Children's Garden is a haven for young explorers, featuring interactive play areas and educational experiences.

Essential Tips and Information:

- **Operating Hours:** Check the official website for current opening hours, admission fees, and guided tour details.
- **Seasonal Variation:** The garden's appearance changes with the seasons, so consider visiting during different times of the year.
- **Photography:** Bring your camera to capture the beauty of the gardens and the unique plant specimens.

Getting There:

- **Public Transit:** The garden is accessible by public transit, with nearby bus stops.
- **Driving:** If driving, the garden has parking facilities available.

The VanDusen Botanical Garden is a garden for nature enthusiasts, a source of inspiration for artists, and a haven of tranquility for those seeking respite from city life. Whether you're strolling through themed gardens, admiring the seasonal blooms, or simply reveling in the peaceful ambiance, the garden invites you to connect with the beauty and diversity of the plant world. As you wander its pathways, breathe in its scents, and soak in its serenity, let the VanDusen Botanical Garden cultivate a sense of wonder, deepen your appreciation for the natural world, and remind you of the intricate beauty that surrounds us.

Queen Elizabeth Theatre

Nestled in the heart of downtown Vancouver, the Queen Elizabeth Theatre is a cultural cornerstone that has been enchanting audiences for decades with its captivating performances and architectural elegance. As a venue for a diverse range of artistic expressions, from theater to ballet and music, this iconic theatre invites patrons to experience the magic of live performances in a setting that exudes sophistication and grandeur.

Address and GPS Position: Queen Elizabeth Theatre, 630 Hamilton St, Vancouver, BC V6B 5N6, Canada
  GPS Coordinates: 49.2795° N, 123.1137° W

Upon entering the Queen Elizabeth Theatre, you'll be greeted by a grand foyer that sets the stage for an evening of cultural enrichment. The theatre's striking design, characterized by its sleek lines and modernist aesthetic, provides an elegant backdrop for a wide range of performances.

A Venue for the Arts: *Theater Productions:* The theatre hosts a variety of theatrical productions, from classic plays and contemporary dramas to musicals that transport audiences to other worlds.

Music Performances: Whether it's a symphony orchestra, a renowned soloist, or a contemporary band, the Queen Elizabeth Theatre serves as a premier destination for musical performances.

Ballet and Dance: The theatre's stage also comes alive with the grace and artistry of ballet and dance companies, showcasing the beauty of movement and expression.

Superior Acoustics: Renowned for its exceptional acoustics, the Queen Elizabeth Theatre ensures that every note, word, and sound resonates with clarity and brilliance, providing an immersive auditory experience.

Essential Tips and Information:

- **Performance Schedule:** Check the official website for the theatre's performance schedule, ticket information, and seating plans.
- **Dress Code:** While there's no strict dress code, many patrons

choose to dress smartly for evening performances.

- **Arrival Time:** Arrive early to allow time for parking, ticket pickup, and to enjoy the atmosphere of the theatre.

Getting There:

- **Public Transit:** The theatre is accessible by public transit, with nearby bus stops and SkyTrain stations.
- **Driving:** If driving, consider using nearby parking facilities or metered street parking.

Whether you're moved by a powerful soliloquy, swept away by a musical crescendo, or transported by a dancer's grace, the theatre offers an opportunity to immerse yourself in the magic of live performances. As you sit in its audience, surrounded by fellow art enthusiasts, let the Queen Elizabeth Theatre remind you of the transformative power of the arts, the universality of human expression, and the connection that the stage fosters between artists and appreciative souls.

Robson Street

Situated in the heart of downtown Vancouver, Robson Street stands as a bustling hub of shopping, dining, and entertainment that captures the city's vibrant urban spirit. Known for its eclectic mix of fashion boutiques, international eateries, and lively street scenes, this iconic street invites visitors to explore its offerings, indulge in culinary delights, and soak in the energy of urban life.

Address and GPS Position: Robson Street, Vancouver, BC, Canada
GPS Coordinates: 49.2821° N, 123.1214° W

Robson Street is renowned for its diverse array of shops and boutiques, offering everything from high-end fashion brands to unique local designs. Explore the latest fashion trends, discover hidden gems, and indulge in a retail therapy experience like no other.

Global Gastronomy: *International Cuisine:* As you stroll along Robson Street, you'll encounter an enticing array of international eateries and restaurants. From Japanese ramen to Italian pasta, the street is a culinary journey that reflects Vancouver's multiculturalism.

Entertainment and Events: *Street Performers:* The vibrant atmosphere of Robson Street often attracts street performers who captivate audiences with their talents, adding to the urban energy.

Coffee Culture and Cafés: *Café Culture:* Immerse yourself in Vancouver's coffee culture by visiting the many cafés that dot Robson Street. Enjoy a cup of locally roasted coffee while people-watching.

Nightlife and Dining: *Evening Vibes:* As the sun sets, Robson Street transforms into a lively destination for nightlife. Explore its diverse range of restaurants, bars, and lounges that offer an evening of entertainment.

Essential Tips and Information:

- **Operating Hours:** Shops, restaurants, and cafés on Robson Street have varying operating hours, so it's recommended to check in advance.
- **Walking Shoes:** Wear comfortable shoes suitable for walking, as Robson Street is best explored on foot.
- **Parking:** Limited parking is available, so consider using public transportation or alternative modes of transport.

Getting There:

- **Public Transit:** Robson Street is accessible by public transit, with several bus routes and SkyTrain stations nearby.
- **Driving:** If driving, nearby parking facilities or metered street parking can be used.

Robson Street invites you to be a part of its dynamic tapestry. As you wander its sidewalks, taste its diverse offerings, and engage with its lively street scenes, let Robson Street inspire your urban exploration and deepen your connection to the vibrant spirit of downtown Vancouver.

Whale Watching in Vancouver

The waters around Vancouver are a playground for some of the world's most magnificent marine creatures. Whale watching in this region offers an awe-inspiring experience as you venture into the Pacific Ocean to witness the breathtaking beauty of whales and other marine wildlife in their natural habitat.

Vancouver's Premier Whale Watching Destinations: *Johnstone Strait:* Known as a prime location for orca (killer whale) sightings, Johnstone Strait, off the northern coast of Vancouver Island, offers the opportunity to witness orca pods in their migratory route.

Georgia Strait: This area, between Vancouver Island and the mainland, is frequented by orcas, humpback whales, gray whales, and minke whales. It's a relatively short distance from Vancouver and offers a high chance of spotting these majestic creatures.

Whale Species You Might Encounter: *Orcas (Killer Whales):* Known for their distinctive black and white markings, orcas are a symbol of the Pacific Northwest. You might witness their playful behaviors and social interactions.

Humpback Whales: These massive creatures are known for their acrobatics, often breaching and slapping their tails on the water's surface.

Gray Whales: During their migrations, gray whales pass through the region, offering a chance for close encounters with these gentle giants.

Tour Operators and Guidelines: When embarking on a whale watching tour, it's important to choose a reputable and eco-conscious tour operator that follows responsible wildlife viewing guidelines. These guidelines prioritize the well-being of the animals and their natural environment.

Season and Best Times: Whale watching tours in Vancouver are popular from spring to fall, with peak season typically from May to September. Different species have different migratory patterns, so the best time for sightings can vary.

Essential Tips and Information:

- **Dress in Layers:** Weather conditions can change quickly on the water, so dress in warm layers and bring a waterproof jacket.
- **Binoculars and Cameras:** Bring binoculars and a camera with a telephoto lens to capture distant whale sightings.
- **Sea Sickness:** If you're prone to seasickness, consider taking preventive measures before the tour.
- **Listen to Crew:** Listen to the instructions of the tour crew regarding safety guidelines and respectful behavior around marine wildlife.

An Encounter with Nature's Giants: Whale watching in Vancouver isn't just a tour; it's a chance to connect with the wild and awe-inspiring world that lies beneath the ocean's surface. As you set sail, keep your eyes peeled for the graceful breaches, powerful tail slaps, and gentle glides of these magnificent creatures. With each sighting, you'll not only witness the wonders of the marine world but also gain a deeper appreciation for the need to protect and preserve these incredible animals and their habitats.

Kayaking in False Creek

False Creek, a picturesque inlet nestled in the heart of Vancouver, offers a unique kayaking experience that seamlessly blends urban charm with natural beauty. As you paddle along the tranquil waters of False Creek, you'll have the opportunity to explore Vancouver's iconic skyline, vibrant neighborhoods, and serene waters—all from the intimate perspective of a kayak.

False Creek: An Urban Oasis: False Creek is a seawater inlet that meanders through Vancouver, separating the downtown core from the rest of the city. This vibrant waterway is surrounded by some of the city's most iconic neighborhoods and landmarks, making it a popular destination for both locals and visitors.

Kayaking Amidst Vancouver's Landmarks: *Granville Island:* Launch your kayak from the shores of Granville Island, an artsy enclave known for its bustling public market, artisan studios, and lively atmosphere.

Science World: As you paddle along False Creek, you'll pass by the distinctive geodesic dome of Science World, an iconic science museum that's impossible to miss.

Yaletown and Olympic Village: Kayak through the stylish neighborhood of Yaletown and the modern community of Olympic Village, where you can admire sleek architecture and stunning waterfront views.

Stunning City and Mountain Views: One of the most captivating aspects of kayaking in False Creek is the juxtaposition of the city's skyscrapers against the backdrop of the majestic North Shore

Mountains. As you paddle along, you'll have the chance to soak in breathtaking views that seamlessly blend urban and natural beauty.

Wildlife and Serenity: Despite being located in the heart of the city, False Creek offers moments of tranquility and the potential to encounter local wildlife. Keep an eye out for seabirds, seals, and even the occasional dolphin or porpoise.

Rental and Guided Tours: Various rental shops and tour operators offer kayaking experiences in False Creek. Whether you're a novice or an experienced paddler, guided tours provide insights into the area's history, landmarks, and urban development.

Essential Tips and Information:

- **Dress Appropriately:** Wear comfortable clothing suitable for kayaking, and consider bringing a waterproof jacket.
- **Sun Protection:** Don't forget sunscreen, a hat, and sunglasses to shield yourself from the sun's rays.
- **Safety First:** Follow safety guidelines provided by rental shops or tour operators and be mindful of other watercraft.

Getting There:

- **Public Transit:** False Creek is accessible by public transit, including bus routes and the SkyTrain.
- **Parking:** Limited parking is available in the area, so using public transportation is recommended.

Kayaking in False Creek offers more than just a leisurely paddle; it's a journey of exploration, a way to intimately connect with Vancouver's urban and natural landscapes. As you glide along the water, taking in the city's sights, sounds, and energy, let False Creek remind you of the harmonious coexistence between urban life and the beauty of nature.

Vancouver Maritime Museum

Tucked along the shores of English Bay, the Vancouver Maritime Museum serves as a captivating portal into the world of maritime exploration, trade, and adventure. This cultural gem invites visitors to embark on a journey through seafaring history, marine artifacts, and captivating exhibitions that highlight the integral role of the ocean in shaping Vancouver's past and present.

Address and GPS Position: Vancouver Maritime Museum, 1905 Ogden Ave, Vancouver, BC V6J 1A3, Canada
   GPS Coordinates: 49.2840° N, 123.1517° W

The museum's exhibits are a treasure trove of maritime history, featuring a diverse collection of ship models, navigational instruments, antique maps, and artifacts that offer insights into the world of maritime exploration and trade.

   Steller's Bay Exploration: *Steller's Bay:* This exhibit showcases the life and achievements of Georg Wilhelm Steller, a German naturalist who was part of Vitus Bering's exploration of the North Pacific in the 18th century.

   Historic Vessels: *St. Roch:* One of the museum's most prominent artifacts is the St. Roch, the first vessel to navigate the Northwest Passage from west to east. This historic ship offers a glimpse into the challenges and triumphs of polar exploration.

   Model Ships and Interactive Displays: *Model Ship Gallery:* Explore an impressive collection of model ships that represent various eras, regions, and types of vessels that have graced the world's oceans.

Maritime Art and Culture: *Ocean Stories:** The museum's exhibits delve into various aspects of maritime culture, from the art of navigation to the maritime communities that have shaped the city's identity.

Special Exhibitions and Events: The Vancouver Maritime Museum regularly hosts special exhibitions, lectures, and events that delve into maritime themes, showcasing a dynamic range of topics and perspectives.

Essential Tips and Information:

- **Operating Hours:** Check the official website for the most up-to-date operating hours, admission fees, and exhibition details.
- **Guided Tours:** Consider joining a guided tour to gain deeper insights into the exhibits and their historical significance.

Getting There:

- **Public Transit:** The museum is accessible by public transit, with nearby bus routes and SkyTrain stations.
- **Driving:** Limited parking is available near the museum, and metered street parking can also be used.

The Vancouver Maritime Museum is a tribute to human exploration, innovation, and the indelible connection between communities and the sea. As you explore its exhibits, admire historic vessels, and immerse yourself in the stories of adventurers who braved the open waters, the museum offers a profound appreciation for the ocean's impact on human history. Let the Vancouver Maritime Museum be your guide through seafaring tales, showcasing the courage, tenacity, and boundless curiosity that have shaped the course of human exploration and discovery.

Jericho Beach

Nestled along the shores of English Bay, Jericho Beach stands as a beloved destination that offers a harmonious blend of natural beauty, outdoor activities, and a laid-back beachside atmosphere. With its sweeping views, sandy shores, and abundance of recreational opportunities, this coastal haven invites locals and visitors alike to bask in the sun, explore the outdoors, and revel in the tranquil ambiance of the Pacific coastline.

Address and GPS Position: Jericho Beach, 3941 Point Grey Rd, Vancouver, BC V6R 4P1, Canada
   GPS Coordinates: 49.2734° N, 123.1932° W

Jericho Beach boasts a wide expanse of sandy shoreline, framed by picturesque views of the North Shore Mountains and the shimmering waters of English Bay. This inviting backdrop creates a perfect setting for relaxation and outdoor activities.

Recreational Opportunities: *Beach Volleyball:* The beach features several volleyball courts, inviting visitors to enjoy friendly matches with the stunning ocean as a backdrop.

Picnicking and BBQs: Ample grassy areas with picnic tables and barbecue facilities make Jericho Beach an ideal spot for family gatherings and outdoor meals.

Sailing and Watersports: *Jericho Sailing Centre:* Adjacent to the beach is the Jericho Sailing Centre, a hub for watersport enthusiasts. From kayaking and windsurfing to sailing and stand-up paddleboarding, there's a water activity for every level of adventurer.

Scenic Views and Sunsets: Jericho Beach is renowned for its stunning sunset views. As the sun dips below the horizon, the skies are painted in vibrant hues, creating a serene and captivating scene.

Jericho Park: Jericho Beach is part of Jericho Park, which encompasses lush green spaces, walking paths, and picnic areas. The park provides a refreshing escape from the city's hustle and bustle, offering a place to connect with nature and unwind.

Essential Tips and Information:

- **Parking:** Limited parking is available in the area, so consider carpooling or using public transportation.
- **Dress in Layers:** Coastal weather can be changeable, so dress in layers to stay comfortable.
- **Swimming Safety:** There are lifeguards on duty during the summer months. Check the safety flags and adhere to any posted guidelines.

Getting There:

- **Public Transit:** Jericho Beach is accessible by public transit, with nearby bus routes.
- **Cycling:** Consider cycling to the beach using Vancouver's network of bike paths.

Jericho Beach is a retreat that beckons you to unwind, explore, and embrace the natural beauty of Vancouver's coastline. Whether you're basking in the sun, participating in watersports, or simply watching the waves roll in, the beach offers a serene escape from the city's pace. As you relish in the simplicity of sandy shores and salt-kissed air, let Jericho Beach remind you of the rejuvenating power of nature and the tranquil allure of the Pacific coastline.

Coal Harbour

Nestled between the bustling cityscape of downtown Vancouver and the serene waters of Burrard Inlet, Coal Harbour is a picturesque neighborhood that seamlessly blends urban sophistication with breathtaking natural landscapes. This waterfront enclave offers a harmonious balance between high-end living, outdoor recreation, and stunning views, making it a coveted destination for residents and visitors alike.

Location and GPS Position: Coal Harbour, Vancouver, BC, Canada **GPS Coordinates**: 49.2891° N, 123.1211° W

Stunning Marina and Seaside Living: Coal Harbour is renowned for its marina, which features a multitude of luxury yachts and boats. Strolling along the seawall, you'll be treated to captivating views of sparkling waters and the majestic North Shore Mountains.

Seawall and Outdoor Activities: *Stanley Park Seawall Connection:* The Coal Harbour Seawall connects to Stanley Park, offering a scenic route for walkers, runners, and cyclists to enjoy panoramic vistas of the harbor and beyond.

Jack Poole Plaza and Olympic Cauldron: *Jack Poole Plaza:* This public space is home to the iconic Olympic Cauldron, which was lit during the 2010 Winter Olympics. The plaza is a gathering spot with benches, water features, and greenery.

Fine Dining and Culinary Experiences: *Waterfront Dining:* Coal Harbour is home to an array of upscale restaurants that offer waterfront dining experiences with stunning views of the harbor and mountains.

Luxury Living and Real Estate: Coal Harbour boasts a range of high-end condominiums and luxury apartments that offer residents breathtaking views, proximity to downtown amenities, and access to the natural beauty of the harbor.

Harbor Air Seaplane Terminal: The Harbor Air Seaplane Terminal, located in Coal Harbour, offers scenic seaplane flights that provide a unique perspective of Vancouver's skyline and the surrounding coastal landscapes.

Essential Tips and Information:

- **Walking Shoes:** Wear comfortable shoes suitable for walking along the seawall and exploring the area.
- **Public Spaces:** Enjoy public spaces like Jack Poole Plaza for relaxation and people-watching.
- **Scenic Photography:** Bring a camera to capture the stunning harbor views and urban landscapes.

Getting There:

- **Public Transit:** Coal Harbour is accessible by public transit, including bus routes and the SkyTrain.
- **Walking:** If you're staying in downtown Vancouver, consider walking to Coal Harbour to enjoy its attractions.

Coal Harbour is a microcosm of Vancouver's allure, where luxury living harmonizes with the tranquility of the harbor and the grandeur of nature. Whether you're strolling along the seawall, admiring the marina's yachts, or indulging in waterfront dining, the neighborhood invites you to immerse yourself in its captivating ambiance. As you gaze at the city lights dancing on the water's surface and embrace the sense of calm that comes with being near the sea, let Coal Harbour remind you of the seamless coexistence between urban sophistication and the serenity of coastal landscapes.

Rogers Arena

Rogers Arena, located in the heart of downtown Vancouver, stands as a premier destination that brings together sports, live entertainment, and cultural events under one iconic roof. As the home of the Vancouver Canucks NHL team and a versatile venue for concerts, performances, and shows, Rogers Arena offers an electrifying atmosphere that captivates audiences and sports enthusiasts alike.

Address and GPS Position: Rogers Arena, 800 Griffiths Way, Vancouver, BC V6B 6G1, Canada
   GPS Coordinates: 49.2775° N, 123.1089° W

As the home of the Vancouver Canucks NHL team, Rogers Arena comes alive with the excitement of ice hockey. Join the passionate crowd as they cheer on the Canucks, creating an atmosphere that's a true reflection of the city's love for the sport.

Live Entertainment and Concerts: Beyond sports, Rogers Arena transforms into a world-class entertainment venue, hosting a diverse lineup of concerts, performances, and events featuring international artists and renowned acts.

Versatile Venue: *Rooftop Garden:* The arena features a unique rooftop garden that provides a tranquil escape amidst the urban hustle, complete with native plants and panoramic city views.

Essential Tips and Information:

- **Event Schedule:** Check the official website for the most up-to-date event schedule, ticket information, and seating plans.
- **Arrival Time:** Arrive early to navigate through security, find parking or public transit options, and enjoy the pre-event atmosphere.

Getting There:

- **Public Transit:** Rogers Arena is accessible by public transit, including bus routes and the SkyTrain.
- **Driving:** Limited parking is available in the area, but there are also parking lots nearby.

Rogers Arena is a stage where sports legends are born, musical talents shine, and live performances create lasting memories. Whether you're witnessing the thrill of a hockey game, swaying to the rhythms of your favorite band, or marveling at the production of a live show, the arena's energy and vibrancy are palpable. As you join the chorus of cheers, immerse yourself in the sensory experiences, and share in the collective excitement, let Rogers Arena remind you of the power of live entertainment to unite people and create moments that stay with you long after the final applause.

Bard on the Beach

Bard on the Beach, an annual cultural gem in Vancouver, brings the timeless works of William Shakespeare to life against the stunning backdrop of the city's waterfront. With its open-air stages, captivating performances, and the rhythmic lapping of waves nearby, this festival creates a magical atmosphere that transports audiences into the world of the Bard's classic plays.

Location and GPS Position: Bard on the Beach, Vanier Park, 1000 Chestnut St, Vancouver, BC V6J 5E1, Canada
GPS Coordinates: 49.2746° N, 123.1377° W

Held in the picturesque Vanier Park, Bard on the Beach offers an immersive experience as audiences gather under open skies to enjoy the works of Shakespeare. The festival stages are designed to complement the natural beauty of the setting, enhancing the storytelling with a touch of outdoor magic.

Playbill Variety: Each season, Bard on the Beach presents a selection of Shakespeare's plays, ranging from beloved classics like "Romeo and Juliet" and "Hamlet" to lesser-known gems that surprise and delight audiences.

Scenic Waterfront Views: While attending a performance at Bard on the Beach, patrons are treated to breathtaking views of the ocean, the mountains, and Vancouver's iconic skyline, creating a truly unique and enchanting theatrical experience.

Charming Village and Atmosphere: The festival grounds are reminiscent of a lively village, complete with pre-show entertainment, concession stands, and opportunities to connect with fellow theatergoers.

Essential Tips and Information:

- **Performance Schedule:** Check the official website for the current season's performance schedule, ticket availability, and showtimes.
- **Outdoor Comfort:** Bring warm layers, blankets, and cushions to ensure your comfort during evening performances.

Getting There:

- **Public Transit:** Bard on the Beach is accessible by public transit, including bus routes and the False Creek Ferries.
- **Driving:** Limited parking is available at Vanier Park, but alternatives such as cycling or public transportation are recommended.

An Open-Air Theatrical Journey: Bard on the Beach is a journey that transports you back in time to Shakespeare's world, where love, tragedy, and human nature take center stage. As you watch the characters come to life against the backdrop of Vancouver's natural beauty, let the rhythm of the waves and the magic of the words envelop you. Bard on the Beach offers a reminder that great stories are timeless, and when they're performed in such a captivating setting, they become a shared experience that transcends generations and brings the power of Shakespeare to life in a whole new light.

Music Festivals

Music festivals are immersive experiences that unite music enthusiasts, artists, and cultures through the universal language of melody and rhythm. These vibrant gatherings offer a unique blend of live performances, artistic expression, and a sense of community that transcends boundaries. From iconic headliners to emerging talents, music festivals create an electric atmosphere that resonates with the hearts of attendees.

Diverse Genres and Themes: Music festivals span a wide spectrum of genres, from rock, pop, and electronic dance music to jazz, folk, classical, and more. Some festivals focus on a specific genre, while others celebrate a diverse mix of musical styles.

Connection and Community: Music festivals create a sense of camaraderie among attendees who share a passion for music. The festival grounds become a haven for self-expression, unity, and a shared appreciation for the artistry of live performances.

Discovery of New Artists: Festivals provide a platform for both established and emerging artists to showcase their talents. Attendees often stumble upon new favorites, fostering an environment of musical exploration and discovery.

Cultural Fusion: Many music festivals go beyond music, incorporating cultural elements such as art installations, culinary experiences, and workshops that celebrate the diversity of the human experience.

Celebration of Creativity: Festivals often feature art installations, interactive exhibits, and immersive environments that engage the senses and spark creativity in attendees.

Global Appeal: From the Coachella Valley Music and Arts Festival in California to Glastonbury Festival in the UK and Tomorrowland in Belgium, music festivals attract attendees from around the world, showcasing the universal appeal of music.

Outdoor and Indoor Venues: Music festivals take place in a variety of settings, from vast open fields to urban parks, beaches, and city centers. Each venue contributes to the festival's unique ambiance and vibe.

Environmental Awareness: Many modern festivals emphasize eco-conscious practices, promoting sustainability, recycling, and reducing environmental impact.

Essential Tips and Information:

- **Tickets:** Purchase tickets in advance, as festivals often sell out quickly.
- **Comfort:** Wear comfortable clothing and footwear suitable for the weather and outdoor conditions.
- **Hydration and Sun Protection:** Stay hydrated and use sunscreen to ensure a comfortable festival experience.

Music festivals are not just gatherings; they are celebrations of life, creativity, and the power of music to inspire, heal, and unite. Whether you're dancing to the rhythm, singing along with the crowd, or simply soaking in the vibrant atmosphere, music festivals offer a momentary escape from the ordinary and a chance to immerse yourself in a world of sonic beauty. As you stand shoulder to shoulder with fellow music lovers, let the melodies wash over you, the collective energy envelop you, and the shared experience remind you of the harmonious threads that connect us all.

Outdoor Movies

Outdoor movies combine the timeless allure of film with the enchantment of open-air settings, creating memorable and immersive movie-watching experiences. From parks and beaches to rooftops and courtyards, these screenings bring people together to enjoy classic films, recent releases, and cinematic gems while surrounded by the beauty of nature or urban landscapes.

Community Gatherings and Entertainment: Outdoor movies foster a sense of community as people of all ages come together to enjoy a shared cinematic experience. Families, friends, and neighbors gather to relax, laugh, and connect over their favorite films.

Diverse Venues: Outdoor movies are hosted in a variety of locations, ranging from public parks and beaches to botanical gardens, amphitheaters, and even urban rooftops.

Picnics and Food Trucks: Many outdoor movie events encourage attendees to bring picnic blankets, cushions, and snacks. Some screenings feature food trucks and concessions, adding to the festive atmosphere.

Nostalgia and Classic Films: Outdoor movie events often showcase beloved classics that evoke nostalgia and transport audiences back to a different era.

Themed Screenings: Some outdoor movie events have themes, such as 80s movies, family-friendly films, or films that align with a particular cultural or seasonal celebration.

Celestial Ambiance: As the sun sets and the stars emerge, the outdoor movie experience is enhanced by the natural backdrop of the night sky.

Cultural and Artistic Fusion: Certain outdoor movie events incorporate live performances, art installations, or music to create a multi-sensory experience that goes beyond the screen.

Essential Tips and Information:

- **Seating:** Bring comfortable seating such as blankets, cushions, or portable chairs.
- **Layers:** Dress in layers to stay warm as temperatures can drop in the evening.
- **Picnic Supplies:** Pack snacks, drinks, and any additional items you need for a comfortable viewing experience.

Getting There:

- **Location-Specific:** Check the event's website for information on location, transportation options, and parking.

Outdoor movies transform film viewing into a communal celebration where cinematic moments are shared in an open-air, relaxed environment. Whether you're snuggled under a blanket or lounging on a beach towel, the experience is a unique blend of nostalgia, creativity, and the joy of storytelling. As you watch the screen illuminate against the night sky, surrounded by laughter and the company of fellow moviegoers, let the magic of outdoor movies remind you of the simple pleasure of coming together to appreciate the art of film beneath the celestial canopy.

Whistler: A Wonderland of Nature and Adventure

Nestled in the heart of the Coast Mountains, Whistler stands as a majestic haven that beckons adventurers, nature enthusiasts, and seekers of all kinds. With its breathtaking landscapes, world-class ski slopes, and year-round outdoor pursuits, Whistler is a destination that captivates the soul and invites exploration like no other.

Location and GPS Position: Whistler, British Columbia, Canada

GPS Coordinates: 50.1163° N, 122.9574° W

Skiing and Snowboarding Paradise: Whistler is renowned for its iconic ski resort, Whistler Blackcomb, where powdery slopes and pristine trails invite winter sports enthusiasts to carve their way down the mountainside. The sheer expanse of the resort, combined with its modern amenities, creates an unparalleled skiing and snowboarding experience.

Summer Splendors: When the snow melts, Whistler transforms into a summer playground, offering hiking trails that wind through old-growth forests, sparkling lakes for kayaking and swimming, and mountain biking trails that challenge and inspire.

Village Vibrancy: The pedestrian-friendly Whistler Village exudes an atmosphere of alpine charm and cosmopolitan energy. Boutiques, galleries, restaurants, and cafés line the cobblestone streets, inviting visitors to indulge in both leisure and entertainment.

Peak 2 Peak Gondola: The Peak 2 Peak Gondola, an engineering marvel, connects Whistler and Blackcomb Mountains, offering panoramic vistas that showcase the grandeur of the surrounding landscapes.

Whistler Olympic Plaza: Built for the 2010 Winter Olympics, the Olympic Plaza is a hub of culture and community events. It features an outdoor stage, a reflecting pond, and a year-round gathering space.

Wildlife Encounters: Whistler's wilderness is home to diverse

71

wildlife, including black bears, deer, and eagles. Guided tours offer opportunities to observe these creatures in their natural habitats.

Essential Tips and Information:

- **Seasonal Attire:** Pack appropriate clothing for the season, whether it's skiing gear or hiking apparel.
- **Reservations:** Book accommodations, dining, and activities in advance, especially during peak seasons.
- **Transportation:** Whistler is accessible by car, bus, or the Whistler Mountaineer train.

Getting There:

- **Driving:** Whistler is a scenic drive from Vancouver along the Sea-to-Sky Highway.
- **Public Transit:** Buses run regularly between Vancouver and Whistler, offering a convenient option.

An Adventure Awaits: Whistler is more than a destination; it's an invitation to embrace the raw beauty of the mountains, the thrill of exploration, and the serenity of the great outdoors. It's a place where the rush of a downhill run is matched only by the tranquility of a lakeside sunset. From the exhilaration of conquering new heights to the comfort of sipping hot cocoa in a cozy café, Whistler offers a symphony of experiences that resonate with your spirit. As you immerse yourself in its natural wonders and connect with its vibrant community, let Whistler be a testament to the power of nature to invigorate, inspire, and leave an indelible mark on your soul.

Bowen Island

Nestled in the emerald waters of Howe Sound, Bowen Island stands as a serene and picturesque retreat that offers a peaceful respite from the bustling city of Vancouver. With its lush landscapes, charming village atmosphere, and outdoor adventures, Bowen Island captures the essence of West Coast living and invites visitors to unwind, explore, and connect with nature.

Location and GPS Position: Bowen Island, British Columbia, Canada
GPS Coordinates: 49.3803° N, 123.3729° W

Bowen Island is a haven for outdoor enthusiasts. Hiking trails crisscross the island, leading to viewpoints that reveal breathtaking vistas of Howe Sound, nearby islands, and the coastal mountains.

Snug Cove Village: The heart of Bowen Island is Snug Cove Village, a charming waterfront community that offers boutiques, galleries, restaurants, and cafés. Strolling along the marina and taking in the picturesque harbor views is a must.

Art and Culture: Bowen Island's creative spirit is evident in its art galleries, studios, and cultural events. The island's community nurtures artistic expression and often hosts exhibitions and workshops.

Dorman Point and Mount Gardner: Hiking to Dorman Point and Mount Gardner rewards you with panoramic views that stretch from the city of Vancouver to the Gulf Islands. These trails are a testament to the island's natural beauty and rugged terrain.

Cates Hill and Artisan Square: Cates Hill offers a unique perspective of Snug Cove and the surrounding landscapes. Nearby Artisan Square is a hub for artisan shops, studios, and culinary delights.

Essential Tips and Information:

- **Ferry Reservations:** Consider making reservations for the ferry to Bowen Island, especially during peak travel times.
- **Weather Preparedness:** Dress in layers and pack appropriate clothing for the weather, as conditions can change quickly.

Getting There:

- **Ferry:** Bowen Island is accessible by ferry from Horseshoe Bay in West Vancouver. The ferry ride itself offers stunning views of Howe Sound.

Bowen Island isn't just an island; it's an invitation to step back from the frenetic pace of everyday life and embrace the tranquility of nature. It's a place where hiking trails lead to awe-inspiring vistas, where charming streets offer delightful surprises, and where the gentle lapping of waves soothes your soul. As you explore the island's natural wonders, engage with its creative community, and bask in the simple pleasures of island life, let Bowen Island remind you of the rejuvenating power of natural beauty and the art of savoring life's small moments.

Victoria: A Majestic Blend of Elegance and Nature

Situated at the southern tip of Vancouver Island, Victoria, the capital city of British Columbia, is a gem that exudes timeless charm, historic significance, and a seamless fusion of natural beauty and urban sophistication. With its lush gardens, stunning architecture, and picturesque waterfront, Victoria offers a captivating escape that celebrates both history and the wonders of the West Coast.

Location and GPS Position: Victoria, British Columbia, Canada

GPS Coordinates: 48.4284° N, 123.3656° W

Inner Harbour and Empress Hotel: The Inner Harbour serves as Victoria's iconic centerpiece, where the majestic Fairmont Empress Hotel commands attention. Its grand architecture and stunning waterfront location create a postcard-worthy scene.

Butchart Gardens: A short drive from downtown Victoria, Butchart Gardens is a horticultural masterpiece that showcases meticulously manicured landscapes, vibrant flowerbeds, and tranquil pathways. It's a feast for the senses in every season.

Royal BC Museum: Explore British Columbia's rich history, indigenous cultures, and natural wonders at the Royal BC Museum, where engaging exhibits and artifacts come to life.

High Tea and Culinary Delights: Indulge in the British tradition of high tea at establishments like the Fairmont Empress, or explore the city's diverse culinary scene that boasts farm-to-table delights and international flavors.

Craigdarroch Castle: This Victorian-era mansion offers a glimpse into the opulent lifestyles of the past. Wander through its ornate rooms and corridors to experience a bygone era of elegance.

Beacon Hill Park: A sprawling urban oasis, Beacon Hill Park is a serene retreat that features manicured gardens, meandering paths, and resident peacocks.

Whale Watching and Waterfront Strolls: Victoria's coastal location offers ample opportunities for whale watching tours, harbor cruises, and leisurely strolls along the waterfront to enjoy the ocean breeze.

Essential Tips and Information:

- **Ferry or Flight:** Access Victoria via a scenic ferry ride from the

mainland or a short flight to the Victoria International Airport.
- **Weather:** Victoria's mild climate makes it a year-round destination, but be prepared for occasional rain even in the warmer months.

Getting There:

- **Ferry:** Ferries from Tsawwassen (Vancouver) to Swartz Bay (Victoria) offer a scenic journey across the Salish Sea.
- **Flight:** Victoria International Airport connects to major cities with regular flights.

Victoria isn't just a city; it's an exquisite blend of regal charm and natural beauty that beckons you to explore its historic streets, revel in its garden splendor, and embrace the coastal tranquility that defines the West Coast. From sipping tea in ornate parlors to marveling at floral displays that rival the rainbow's hues, Victoria invites you to experience the harmony between human creativity and the enchanting landscapes that surround it. As you wander through its historic sites, immerse yourself in its cultural richness, and relish in the warm embrace of its maritime atmosphere, let Victoria remind you that beauty can be found in every corner, and every step is a discovery waiting to unfold.

Squamish

Nestled between the coastal city of Vancouver and the outdoor playground of Whistler, Squamish is a gateway to exhilarating adventures and breathtaking landscapes. From rugged mountains and lush forests to adrenaline-pumping activities, Squamish captures the essence of British Columbia's wild beauty and spirit of exploration.

Location and GPS Position: Squamish, British Columbia, Canada
GPS Coordinates: 49.7000° N, 123.1483° W

Squamish is an outdoor enthusiast's dream come true. It's renowned for rock climbing, offering world-class routes that challenge climbers of all levels. The Stawamus Chief, a towering granite monolith, is an iconic climbing destination.

Sea-to-Sky Gondola: The Sea-to-Sky Gondola offers stunning panoramic views of Howe Sound, coastal mountains, and dense forests. The Sky Pilot Suspension Bridge provides an awe-inspiring perspective of the landscape.

Hiking and Biking Trails: Squamish boasts an extensive network of hiking and mountain biking trails that wind through ancient forests, past waterfalls, and up to breathtaking viewpoints.

Shannon Falls Provincial Park: Visit Shannon Falls, one of the tallest waterfalls in British Columbia. A short hike leads to viewpoints that allow you to witness the cascading beauty up close.

Squamish Spit and Kiteboarding: The Squamish Spit is a mecca for kiteboarders and windsurfers. Its strong winds and shallow waters create the perfect conditions for these thrilling water sports.

Brackendale Eagles Provincial Park: During the winter, Brackendale Eagles Provincial Park becomes a haven for bald eagles that congregate along the Squamish River. Witnessing these majestic birds in their natural habitat is a remarkable experience.

Essential Tips and Information:

- **Weather Preparedness:** Squamish's weather can change quickly. Dress in layers and be prepared for rain.
- **Adventure Gear:** Bring appropriate gear for outdoor activities, including sturdy footwear, rain jackets, and sun protection.

Getting There:

- **Driving:** Squamish is accessible by car via the Sea-to-Sky Highway (Highway 99), offering a scenic drive.
- **Public Transit:** Buses connect Squamish with Vancouver and other nearby towns.

Squamish is an invitation to embrace the rugged landscapes, seek adventure, and forge unforgettable memories. From the thrill of conquering climbing routes to the tranquility of hiking through old-growth forests, the town is a testament to the boundless wonders of the Pacific Northwest. As you gaze upon panoramic vistas, feel the wind against your skin, and immerse yourself in the raw beauty that surrounds you, let Squamish remind you of the unbreakable bond between humans and nature, and the exhilarating sense of freedom that comes with exploring the great outdoors.

Harrison Hot Springs: A Relaxing Retreat of Thermal Tranquility

Nestled in the Fraser Valley of British Columbia, Harrison Hot Springs is a serene oasis that invites visitors to immerse themselves in soothing thermal waters, picturesque landscapes, and a sense of tranquility that comes from being enveloped in nature's embrace. With its natural hot springs, outdoor activities, and small-town charm, Harrison Hot Springs offers a rejuvenating escape from the demands of everyday life.

Location and GPS Position: Harrison Hot Springs, British Columbia, Canada
GPS Coordinates: 49.3032° N, 121.7816° W

Natural Hot Springs and Healing Waters: Harrison Hot Springs is renowned for its natural hot springs, where mineral-rich waters flow from deep within the earth, offering a therapeutic and relaxing experience. The hot springs are the heart of the town's allure.

Harrison Lake: Harrison Lake's crystal-clear waters offer opportunities for swimming, kayaking, fishing, and boating. The lakeside setting is a serene backdrop for unwinding and enjoying the great outdoors.

Hiking and Nature Trails: The area surrounding Harrison Hot Springs features hiking trails that wind through lush forests and lead to stunning viewpoints, offering an opportunity to connect with nature.

Village Charm and Artisan Shops: The village of Harrison Hot Springs exudes a quaint charm with its artisan boutiques, galleries, and local shops. Strolling along the streets and exploring unique finds is a delightful pastime.

Harrison Festival of the Arts: This annual event celebrates the cultural diversity of the region through music, art, dance, and performances from around the world.

Sasquatch Provincial Park: Located nearby, Sasquatch Provincial Park offers opportunities for camping, hiking, and enjoying the serenity of nature. Hicks Lake and its sandy beaches are perfect for picnicking and swimming.

Essential Tips and Information:

- **Hot Springs Reservations:** Consider making reservations for the hot springs in advance, especially during peak times.
- **Water Activities:** Bring appropriate attire for water activities and sun protection.

Getting There:

- **Driving:** Harrison Hot Springs is accessible by car, approximately a 90-minute drive from Vancouver.
- **Public Transit:** Buses connect the region with Vancouver and other nearby towns.

A Thermal Haven of Tranquility: Harrison Hot Springs is a place where time slows down, stresses melt away, and the soothing waters of the hot springs work their magic on body and soul. From leisurely lakeside moments to exploring scenic trails, the town offers a sanctuary for those seeking solace in nature's beauty. As you soak in the healing waters, gaze upon breathtaking vistas, and savor the simplicity of life by the lake, let Harrison Hot Springs remind you of the innate connection between natural elements and well-being, and the profound sense of relaxation that comes from immersing yourself in the gentle embrace of thermal waters.

Richmond Night Market

The Richmond Night Market is a lively and vibrant summer tradition that transforms the evenings into a carnival of sights, sounds, and flavors. Located in the bustling city of Richmond, British Columbia, this annual market captivates visitors with its eclectic mix of street food, unique merchandise, entertainment, and cultural experiences, making it a must-visit destination for both locals and tourists.

Location and GPS Position: Richmond Night Market, 8351 River Rd, Richmond, BC V6X 1Y4, Canada
  GPS Coordinates: 49.1823° N, 123.1316° W

The Richmond Night Market draws inspiration from the vibrant night markets found across Asia, offering a fusion of cultures, cuisines, and entertainment that reflects the diversity of the region.

Diverse Street Food Delights: Food lovers rejoice as the night market showcases a tantalizing array of street food stalls offering a medley of international flavors, from classic Asian dishes to innovative fusion creations.

Merchant Tents and Artisanal Finds: Explore merchant tents that offer a variety of goods, from clothing and accessories to unique crafts and cultural treasures, making it a great place for souvenir hunting.

Entertainment and Performances: The night market comes alive with live entertainment, including musical performances, cultural shows, and interactive activities that engage visitors of all ages.

Magical Atmosphere: As the sun sets, the night market illuminates with colorful lights, lanterns, and a festive ambiance that sets the stage for an unforgettable evening of exploration and enjoyment.

Family-Friendly Activities: The Richmond Night Market caters to families with rides, games, and interactive areas for children, creating a welcoming environment for all generations.

Essential Tips and Information:

- **Cash and Cards:** Bring cash for small transactions, as some stalls might not accept cards.
- **Comfortable Footwear:** Wear comfortable shoes suitable for walking, as you'll be exploring the market grounds.

Getting There:

- **Driving:** Richmond Night Market is accessible by car, with parking available on-site and in nearby areas.
- **Public Transit:** Buses and the SkyTrain connect Richmond Night Market with various parts of Metro Vancouver.

A Night of Culinary and Cultural Exploration: The Richmond Night Market is an immersive experience that transports you to a world of tantalizing flavors, captivating performances, and a festive atmosphere that sparks joy. As you wander through the bustling stalls, indulge in mouthwatering treats, and absorb the vibrant energy that surrounds you, let the night market remind you of the power of cultural exchange, the joy of discovery, and the ability of a single event to bring people together to celebrate life, community, and the simple pleasure of exploring the world one bite at a time.

West End Farmers Market

The West End Farmers Market, nestled in the heart of Vancouver's West End neighborhood, is a vibrant gathering that celebrates the joys of local produce, artisanal goods, and the warm embrace of community. This weekly market showcases the bounty of the region while creating a space for neighbors, visitors, and vendors to connect, share stories, and revel in the simple pleasures of fresh and wholesome offerings.

Location and GPS Position: West End Farmers Market, Comox St & Bute St, Vancouver, BC V6E 4E3, Canada
   GPS Coordinates: 49.2869° N, 123.1303° W

The market features a variety of stalls offering farm-fresh fruits, vegetables, herbs, and more, giving visitors the opportunity to support local agriculture while indulging in seasonal delights.

Artisanal Goods and Crafts: Beyond produce, the market showcases an array of artisanal products, including handmade crafts, baked goods, preserves, cheeses, and ethically sourced meats.

Community Gathering: The West End Farmers Market fosters a sense of community as neighbors and friends gather to peruse the stalls, catch up on local news, and build connections with the farmers and producers.

Live Music and Entertainment: Live music performances, buskers, and interactive activities contribute to the lively atmosphere, creating an environment that's both festive and welcoming.

Educational Opportunities: The market often hosts workshops, demonstrations, and educational sessions that promote sustainable practices, healthy eating, and the importance of supporting local growers.

Diverse Cuisine and Food Trucks: Food trucks and stalls offer a wide range of cuisine, from global flavors to locally inspired dishes, making it a hub for culinary exploration.

Essential Tips and Information:

- **Reusable Bags:** Bring your own reusable bags to carry your purchases and reduce waste.
- **Cash and Cards:** While many vendors accept cards, it's a good idea to have some cash on hand for small transactions.

Getting There:

- **Walking:** If you're in the West End neighborhood, you can easily walk to the market.
- **Public Transit:** Buses and the SkyTrain provide convenient access to the West End Farmers Market.

The West End Farmers Market isn't just a place to shop; it's a gathering that embodies the spirit of community, connection, and sustainability. As you stroll through the vibrant stalls, engage with passionate vendors, and savor the tastes of the season, let the market remind you of the importance of supporting local producers, cultivating relationships, and reveling in the beauty of a shared experience that celebrates the simple joys of food, friendship, and the vibrant tapestry of the West End neighborhood.

Culinary Tours in Vancouver

Culinary tours in Vancouver offer a delectable journey through the city's diverse flavors, vibrant food scene, and cultural richness. From food trucks and hidden gems to upscale dining experiences, these tours immerse you in the culinary tapestry of Vancouver, revealing the stories, traditions, and creative innovations that make the city a true food lover's paradise.

Diverse Neighborhoods and Cuisines: Vancouver's culinary tours often explore a range of neighborhoods, each with its unique culinary identity. From the bustling streets of Chinatown to the trendy vibes of Gastown and the multicultural markets of Granville Island, you'll sample a medley of cuisines.

Food Trucks and Street Eats: Vancouver is renowned for its food truck scene, and culinary tours often take you on a journey to savor gourmet street food. Indulge in innovative twists on classic dishes, international flavors, and locally sourced ingredients.

Local Artisans and Markets: Many tours include visits to local markets where you can interact with vendors, taste fresh produce, artisanal cheeses, and homemade pastries. Granville Island Public Market is a highlight, offering an array of gourmet delights.

Ethnic Flavors and Fusion Cuisine: Vancouver's multicultural makeup is reflected in its culinary scene. Enjoy a fusion of flavors from around the world, whether it's Japanese-inspired cuisine, Middle Eastern delicacies, or creative West Coast fusion.

Farm-to-Table Experiences: Vancouver's proximity to fertile farmlands and the ocean results in exceptional farm-to-table dining experiences. Some tours offer visits to farms or seafood markets, providing insight into the ingredients that grace your plate.

Culinary Workshops and Demonstrations: Some tours go beyond tasting and offer hands-on culinary experiences. Engage in cooking workshops, learn from skilled chefs, and gain insights into the art of crafting exquisite dishes.

Local Craft Beverages: Vancouver's craft beer, wine, and spirits scene is a significant part of its culinary culture. Some tours include stops at local breweries, wineries, and distilleries, allowing you to savor the region's finest libations.

Essential Tips and Information:

- **Appetite:** Come hungry and ready to indulge in a variety of tastings.
- **Comfortable Shoes:** Wear comfortable walking shoes, as culinary tours often involve exploration on foot.

Booking a Culinary Adventure:

- **Online:** Many tour companies offer online booking and provide details about the tour's itinerary and inclusions.

A Flavorful Exploration of Vancouver's Culinary Identity: Culinary tours in Vancouver aren't just about tasting food; they're an immersive journey that connects you with the heart and soul of the city's food culture. As you sample a diverse array of dishes, engage with local artisans, and uncover hidden gems, let the culinary tours remind you that food is more than sustenance—it's a gateway to culture, a way to celebrate community, and an opportunity to savor life's simple pleasures in every delicious bite.

(CHECK OUT "WHERE TO EAT" IN THE COMING CHAPTER)

Commodore Ballroom

The Commodore Ballroom, nestled in the heart of Vancouver, stands as a legendary music venue that has left an indelible mark on the city's cultural landscape. With its storied history, iconic atmosphere, and exceptional acoustics, the Commodore Ballroom has hosted some of the world's most renowned musicians and continues to be a beloved hub of live music and entertainment.

Location and GPS Position: Commodore Ballroom, 868 Granville St, Vancouver, BC V6Z 1K3, Canada
  GPS Coordinates: 49.2794° N, 123.1216° W

Built in 1929, the Commodore Ballroom has witnessed nearly a century of music history. It has served as a dance hall, hosted jazz legends, and evolved into a premiere concert venue.

Iconic Architecture and Interiors: The venue's distinctive art deco architecture, intricate detailing, and spacious ballroom layout contribute to its vintage charm and unique aesthetic.

Superb Acoustics: Renowned for its exceptional sound quality, the Commodore Ballroom's acoustics create an immersive musical experience, making it a favorite among artists and audiences alike.

Legends and Performances: The list of legendary artists who have graced the Commodore's stage is impressive, ranging from Duke Ellington and Count Basie to Nirvana, The Police, and David Bowie.

Diverse Genres and Events: The venue hosts an eclectic array of musical genres, from rock and pop to electronic, jazz, and beyond. It's also a popular spot for dance parties and special events.

Intimate Atmosphere: Despite its capacity, the Commodore Ballroom maintains an intimate vibe that allows concertgoers to feel close to the performers, fostering a connection between artists and their audience.

Essential Tips and Information:

- **Tickets:** Purchase tickets in advance, as shows at the Commodore Ballroom often sell out quickly.
- **Arrival:** Arrive early to secure a good spot, especially if you want to be close to the stage.

Getting There:

- **Transit:** The venue is easily accessible by public transit, with bus stops and SkyTrain stations nearby.
- **Parking:** Limited street parking and nearby parking lots are available for those driving.

The Commodore Ballroom is a living testament to the power of music to shape culture, ignite passion, and create lasting memories. As you step through its doors, surrounded by the echoes of performances that have resonated through generations, let the Commodore Ballroom remind you that music is a timeless force that transcends boundaries, unites souls, and leaves an unforgettable imprint on the heart and soul of a city.

Farmers Markets

Farmers markets are vibrant hubs that celebrate the local harvest, offer a direct connection between producers and consumers, and foster a sense of community that transcends the transactional nature of commerce. These bustling marketplaces showcase the region's agricultural diversity, support local farmers and artisans, and invite visitors to savor the flavors of the season while embracing the charm of an age-old tradition.

Local and Seasonal Delights: Farmers markets highlight the best of what each season has to offer. From freshly picked fruits and vegetables to artisanal cheeses, baked goods, and flowers, the market showcases a medley of local delights.

Supporting Local Producers: By shopping at farmers markets, you support local farmers, growers, and artisans who pour their dedication and expertise into their products. The direct-to-consumer model ensures that a fair portion of the proceeds reaches the people who cultivate the goods.

Culinary Exploration: Farmers markets encourage culinary exploration and experimentation. Try unique heirloom varieties, discover new ingredients, and engage with vendors who are passionate about sharing their knowledge and recipes.

Community Gathering: Farmers markets are more than just places to shop; they're community gathering spaces. They create a welcoming environment where neighbors, friends, and families come together, fostering connections and shared experiences.

Artisanal Crafts and Goods: Many farmers markets feature local artisans who offer handmade crafts, jewelry, textiles, and other unique creations that reflect the region's artistic spirit.

Educational Opportunities: Farmers markets often host workshops, cooking demonstrations, and presentations on topics such as sustainable farming practices, gardening, and food preservation.

Sustainability and Eco-Friendly Practices: Buying local reduces the carbon footprint associated with transporting goods over long distances. Additionally, many vendors at farmers markets practice sustainable farming methods.

Essential Tips and Information:

- **Reusable Bags:** Bring your own reusable bags to carry your purchases and reduce waste.
- **Cash and Cards:** While many vendors accept cards, it's a good idea to have some cash on hand for small transactions.

Finding a Farmers Market:

- **Local Listings:** Check local directories, websites, or community boards for information about farmers markets in your area.

Farmers markets are not just a place to shop; they're a celebration of the harvest, a testament to the dedication of local producers, and a bridge that connects people with the source of their food. As you stroll through the colorful stalls, engage with vendors who pour their hearts into their products, and savor the bounty of the land, let the farmers market remind you of the timeless connection between food, culture, and community—a connection that transcends generations and nourishes the body and soul in every bite.

Yaletown: Urban Chic Meets Historic Charm

Nestled along the waterfront in downtown Vancouver, Yaletown is a trendy and dynamic neighborhood that seamlessly blends urban sophistication with historic character. Once an industrial district, Yaletown has undergone a remarkable transformation to become a vibrant hub of stylish boutiques, upscale dining, and a thriving arts scene, all set against a backdrop of restored heritage buildings and modern skyscrapers.

Location and GPS Position: Yaletown, Vancouver, British Columbia, Canada
   GPS Coordinates: 49.2748° N, 123.1210° W

Yaletown's history is evident in its carefully preserved red-brick warehouses and former industrial sites that have been repurposed into chic lofts, boutiques, and eateries.

   Stylish Boutiques and Galleries: The neighborhood is a haven for shoppers seeking high-end fashion, locally designed jewelry, unique homewares, and contemporary art galleries.

   Waterfront Seating and Parks: Yaletown's proximity to False Creek offers picturesque waterfront views and inviting parks, making it a popular spot for leisurely strolls, picnics, and outdoor activities.

   Culinary Excellence: Yaletown's restaurant scene is a highlight, offering a diverse range of international cuisines, farm-to-table fare, and innovative gastronomic experiences.

   Vibrant Nightlife: As the sun sets, Yaletown transforms into a lively nightlife district with cocktail lounges, wine bars, and upscale pubs, catering to a diverse crowd.

   Marinas and Waterfront Activities: Yaletown's marinas provide a gateway to water sports and boating activities, making it a hub for kayaking, stand-up paddleboarding, and sailing.

   Annual Events and Festivals: Yaletown hosts a variety of events throughout the year, including cultural festivals, art walks, and outdoor markets that celebrate the neighborhood's vibrancy.

Essential Tips and Information:

- **Walking Shoes:** Comfortable shoes are a must for exploring

Yaletown's streets and waterfront.

- **Parking and Transit:** Public transit is convenient, and parking can be limited, so consider using public transportation.

Getting There:

- **SkyTrain:** Yaletown is easily accessible via the Canada Line SkyTrain, with stations at Yaletown-Roundhouse and Vancouver City Centre.

Yaletown isn't just a neighborhood; it's a canvas that paints a picture of Vancouver's evolution from its industrial roots to its contemporary urban identity. As you wander its stylish streets, dine in its acclaimed eateries, and embrace the juxtaposition of historic architecture and modern design, let Yaletown remind you of the city's ability to reinvent itself while preserving its unique essence—a reminder that every corner holds the promise of discovery, connection, and the beauty of a city that embraces the old and the new in harmonious harmony.

Vancouver TheatreSports League

The Vancouver TheatreSports League (VTSL) is a comedic gem that has been entertaining audiences with spontaneous improvisational performances for decades. Nestled in the heart of Vancouver, this unique theatre company offers a dynamic blend of creativity, humor, and interactive storytelling that brings laughter to the forefront of the entertainment experience.

Location and GPS Position: Vancouver TheatreSports League, 1502 Duranleau St, Vancouver, BC V6H 3S4, Canada

GPS Coordinates: 49.2713° N, 123.1311° W

VTSL specializes in improvisational theatre, where actors create scenes, characters, and stories on the spot based on audience suggestions. The unpredictable nature of improv guarantees a one-of-a-kind performance every time.

The Improv Format: TheatreSports performances typically involve different improv games and formats, where teams of talented improvisers compete in a friendly battle of wits, creativity, and humor.

Interactive Audience Engagement: Audience participation is a key element of VTSL's shows. Audience members provide suggestions that inspire scenes, ensuring that no two performances are alike.

Diverse Themes and Genres: VTSL offers a variety of themed shows, from classic TheatreSports battles to themed performances like murder mysteries, improvised musicals, and parodies of well-known genres.

Comedic Talent and Spontaneity: The improvisers at VTSL are skilled performers who thrive on spontaneity, quick thinking, and the ability to create humor on the spot.

Special Events and Workshops: In addition to regular performances, VTSL offers workshops, classes, and special events that allow participants to explore the art of improvisation and comedy.

Essential Tips and Information:

- **Tickets:** Purchase tickets in advance, especially for popular shows, as VTSL performances often sell out.
- **Arrival:** Arrive early to secure good seats and have time to enjoy pre-show activities.

Getting There:

- **Transit:** VTSL is accessible by public transit, with bus stops and ferry terminals nearby.
- **Parking:** Limited street parking and nearby parking lots are available for those driving.

The Vancouver TheatreSports League isn't just a theatre; it's a haven of unscripted humor and a testament to the magic of human creativity and interaction. As you sit in the audience, engaged with the performers and immersed in the world of spontaneous storytelling, let VTSL remind you that laughter is a universal language that bridges gaps, ignites joy, and reminds us that life's most hilarious moments often arise from the unexpected—a powerful lesson in the art of finding humor in the journey.

Dr. Sun Yat-sen Classical Chinese Garden

Located within Vancouver's bustling Chinatown, the Dr. Sun Yat-sen Classical Chinese Garden stands as a serene and exquisite oasis that pays homage to the timeless traditions of Chinese architecture, horticulture, and cultural heritage. This authentic classical garden transports visitors to another world, inviting them to explore a tranquil space that reflects the delicate balance between nature, aesthetics, and human connection.

Location and GPS Position: Dr. Sun Yat-sen Classical Chinese Garden, 578 Carrall St, Vancouver, BC V6B 5K2, Canada
   GPS Coordinates: 49.2791° N, 123.1037° W

Cultural Symbolism and Design: The garden's meticulous design is steeped in symbolism, reflecting the balance of yin and yang, the interconnectedness of all elements, and the harmony between nature and human intervention.

Authentic Architecture: The garden boasts traditional Ming Dynasty-style architecture, with intricate wood carvings, vibrant tiles, and elegant pavilions that evoke the architectural charm of ancient China.

Koi-Filled Ponds and Flora: Water features, including koi-filled ponds, meandering streams, and reflective pools, are surrounded by carefully curated flora that showcase the changing seasons in a symphony of colors.

Teahouse and Cultural Programs: The on-site teahouse serves as a hub for cultural activities, where visitors can savor Chinese teas, partake in calligraphy workshops, and engage in discussions about Chinese heritage.

Lantern Festivals and Events: The garden hosts special events, including lantern festivals, performances, and cultural celebrations that provide a deeper understanding of Chinese customs and traditions.

Peaceful Ambiance: Walking through the garden's meandering paths, visitors are enveloped in a sense of tranquility, as the calming sound of flowing water and the gentle rustle of leaves create an atmosphere of serenity.

Community Engagement and Education: The Dr. Sun Yat-sen Classical Chinese Garden serves as a cultural hub, fostering a greater understanding of Chinese history, art, and philosophy among visitors of all backgrounds.

Essential Tips and Information:

- **Guided Tours:** Consider taking a guided tour to gain insights into the garden's history, design, and cultural significance.
- **Photography:** Capture the beauty, but remember that the garden

encourages a mindful, respectful approach to photography.

Getting There:

- **Transit:** The garden is accessible by public transit, with bus stops and SkyTrain stations in close proximity.
- **Walking:** Explore the garden on foot, as it's conveniently located within Chinatown.

A Haven of Cultural Elegance and Tranquility: The Dr. Sun Yat-sen Classical Chinese Garden is a living embodiment of artistic expression, cultural legacy, and the profound connection between humans and nature. As you step into its enchanting world, surrounded by the delicate beauty of its architecture, the soothing embrace of its natural elements, and the rich tapestry of Chinese traditions, let the garden remind you of the universality of beauty, the richness of cultural diversity, and the serenity that can be found in the simplest moments of reflection—a reminder that in the midst of urban life, a tranquil oasis of cultural harmony awaits those who seek it.

Science World at Telus World of Science

Nestled along the waterfront in Vancouver, Science World at Telus World of Science is a captivating and interactive science center that ignites curiosity, engages minds, and celebrates the wonders of exploration. With its iconic geodesic dome and a plethora of immersive exhibits, this dynamic institution encourages visitors of all ages to delve into the fascinating world of science, technology, and innovation.

Location and GPS Position: Science World at Telus World of

Science, 1455 Quebec St, Vancouver, BC V6A 3Z7, Canada GPS Coordinates: 49.2737° N, 123.1039° W

Interactive Learning Experiences: The science center offers hands-on exhibits and interactive displays that cater to various interests, from physics and biology to chemistry and space exploration.

OMNIMAX Theatre: The OMNIMAX theatre showcases breathtaking films on a massive screen, creating an immersive cinematic experience that transports audiences to various corners of the world.

Themes and Galleries: Science World's galleries cover a range of themes, including ecosystems, human anatomy, physics, technology, and the natural world, inviting visitors to explore diverse realms of knowledge.

Feature Exhibitions: The center hosts rotating feature exhibitions that delve into specific scientific topics, providing in-depth insights and interactive experiences.

Curious Kids Gallery: Designed for younger visitors, this space sparks early interest in science through age-appropriate exhibits and activities.

Outdoor Science Park: The center's outdoor space features interactive installations, including a water play area, giant musical instruments, and physics-based exhibits.

Live Science Demonstrations: Regular live science demonstrations and interactive presentations engage visitors with fun experiments and captivating displays of scientific principles.

Community Engagement and Outreach: Science World is committed to fostering a love for learning beyond its walls, with educational outreach programs, workshops, and events.

Essential Tips and Information:

- **Tickets:** Purchase tickets online or at the venue. Consider

membership options for unlimited access and special benefits.
- **Operating Hours:** Check the center's website for current operating hours, as they may vary.

Getting There:

- **Transit:** Science World is accessible by public transit, with bus stops and the SkyTrain station nearby.
- **Parking:** Limited paid parking is available on-site.

A Journey of Discovery and Wonder: Science World at Telus World of Science isn't just a place of learning; it's a testament to the power of human curiosity and the boundless possibilities of scientific exploration. As you wander through its interactive exhibits, watch the dome come alive with educational films, and witness the spark of inspiration in the eyes of young learners, let Science World remind you that the pursuit of knowledge is a never-ending adventure—one that brings us closer to understanding the world, ignites our passion for discovery, and reminds us that the quest for understanding is a journey worth embracing.

Bloedel Conservatory

Perched atop Queen Elizabeth Park, the Bloedel Conservatory is a mesmerizing haven of lush greenery, vibrant flora, and tranquil beauty enclosed within a stunning geodesic dome. This iconic Vancouver attraction offers visitors a captivating escape into a tropical paradise, where diverse plant species thrive in a carefully curated environment that's both educational and enchanting.

Location and GPS Position: Bloedel Conservatory, 4600 Cambie St,

Vancouver, BC V5Y 2M4, Canada
  GPS Coordinates: 49.2415° N, 123.1121° W

Geodesic Dome Splendor: The conservatory's geodesic dome, designed by Buckminster Fuller, is an architectural marvel that houses a flourishing ecosystem under its iconic triangular panels.

Diverse Botanical Collections: Inside the dome, visitors can explore a diverse range of plant collections, from tropical rainforests to arid desert landscapes.

Exotic Flora and Fauna: Bloedel Conservatory is home to a variety of exotic plant species, including colorful orchids, towering palms, delicate ferns, and rare tropical blooms.

Birds of Paradise: The conservatory also houses a vibrant population of exotic birds, including finches, parrots, and quails, adding a lively touch to the lush surroundings.

Year-Round Beauty: One of Bloedel Conservatory's highlights is its year-round beauty. Visitors can escape the winter chill and immerse themselves in a world of vibrant colors and fragrant blooms.

Educational Experience: The conservatory offers educational programs and guided tours that provide insights into the plants, ecology, and conservation efforts that sustain this unique ecosystem.

Sensory Overload: The conservatory engages the senses with the sights, sounds, and scents of a tropical paradise, making it a sensory escape for visitors of all ages.

Essential Tips and Information:

- **Operating Hours:** Check the conservatory's website for current operating hours and any special events.
- **Photography:** Capture the beauty, but be mindful of the birds and plants when taking photos.

Getting There:

- **Transit:** The conservatory is accessible by public transit, with bus stops and SkyTrain stations nearby.
- **Parking:** Limited parking is available on-site, and additional parking can be found nearby.

A Captivating Journey Through Nature's Diversity: The Bloedel Conservatory isn't just a greenhouse; it's a symphony of nature's diversity, an ode to the intricate balance of ecosystems, and a reminder of the magic that can be found within the embrace of the natural world. As you step into its enchanting dome, surrounded by the vibrant hues of tropical flowers, the soothing rustle of leaves, and the gentle songs of exotic birds, let Bloedel Conservatory remind you that within the heart of the city, an oasis of wonder and tranquility awaits—one that celebrates the richness of the Earth's flora and fauna and invites you to explore the beauty of life in its myriad forms.

Lighthouse Park: A Natural Gem of Tranquility and Scenic Beauty

Located on the rugged coastline of West Vancouver, Lighthouse Park stands as a majestic testament to the unspoiled beauty of the Pacific Northwest. This pristine parkland offers visitors a captivating blend of lush rainforests, rugged trails, and breathtaking ocean vistas, all centered around the iconic Point Atkinson Lighthouse that has guided ships for over a century.

Location and GPS Position: Lighthouse Park, Beacon Ln, West Vancouver, BC V7W 1K5, Canada
  GPS Coordinates: 49.3373° N, 123.2743° W

Lighthouse and Maritime History: The historic Point Atkinson Lighthouse, which has been in operation since 1875, is a focal point of the park and provides a glimpse into the region's maritime history.

Coastal Trails and Exploration: Lighthouse Park boasts a network of well-maintained trails that wind through dense rainforests, revealing stunning viewpoints overlooking the rugged coastline and the majestic Strait of Georgia.

Ancient Trees and Flora: The park is home to old-growth Douglas fir and red cedar trees, as well as a diverse range of native flora, making it a haven for nature enthusiasts and photographers.

Eagle Viewing: Lighthouse Park is a prime location for eagle watching, especially during the fall and winter months, as these majestic birds of prey soar above the cliffs and shoreline.

Picnic Areas and Serene Retreats: The park offers several picnic areas where visitors can enjoy a leisurely meal amidst the natural beauty, while secluded benches provide serene spots for contemplation.

Eco-Friendly Practices: Lighthouse Park encourages eco-friendly practices, such as sticking to designated trails, carrying out any waste, and respecting the park's delicate ecosystem.

Essential Tips and Information:

- **Footwear:** Wear sturdy hiking shoes or boots, as some trails can be uneven and muddy.
- **Weather:** Dress in layers, as the weather can change quickly near the coastline.

Getting There:

- **Transit:** Lighthouse Park is accessible by public transit, with bus stops and ferry terminals nearby.
- **Parking:** Limited parking is available on-site, but spaces can fill up quickly on weekends.

A Journey into the Wild Beauty of the Pacific Coast: Lighthouse Park isn't just a park; it's a living symphony of nature's grandeur, an invitation to explore the untamed beauty of the Pacific Coast, and a sanctuary where the ancient rhythm of the land meets the eternal rhythm of the sea. As you traverse its winding trails, stand in awe at its panoramic viewpoints, and feel the salty breeze on your skin, let Lighthouse Park remind you that amidst the modern world, there are still places untouched by time—places where the echoes of the past mingle with the whispers of the ocean, and where every step is a tribute to the majesty of the natural world.

Kerrisdale Village:

Nestled in the heart of Vancouver's West Side, Kerrisdale Village is a delightful neighborhood that exudes a timeless charm, a warm sense of community, and a harmonious blend of local boutiques, eateries, and cultural experiences. This upscale enclave captures the essence of classic elegance while offering a modern twist that makes it a beloved destination for residents and visitors alike.

Location and GPS Position: Kerrisdale Village, Vancouver, BC, Canada

GPS Coordinates: 49.2345° N, 123.1559° W

Quaint Boutiques and Shops: Kerrisdale Village boasts an array of boutique shops, fashion boutiques, specialty stores, and artisanal galleries that offer unique treasures and bespoke items.

Culinary Delights: From cozy cafes to gourmet restaurants, Kerrisdale's culinary scene presents a variety of dining options that cater to diverse tastes and cravings.

Local Markets and Events: The neighborhood hosts farmers markets, art exhibitions, and community events that foster a strong sense of local identity and bring neighbors together.

Streetscape and Architectural Charm: Kerrisdale is characterized by its tree-lined streets, heritage buildings, and a blend of architectural styles that reflect the neighborhood's rich history.

Cultural Enrichment: Kerrisdale's proximity to arts and cultural centers, such as galleries and theaters, ensures that residents and visitors have access to a range of creative experiences.

Green Spaces and Parks: The neighborhood is complemented by lush parks and green spaces, providing places to unwind, stroll, and appreciate the beauty of nature.

A Sense of Community: Kerrisdale Village is known for its strong sense of community, where locals often gather for events, interact with business owners, and enjoy the neighborly atmosphere.

Essential Tips and Information:

- **Parking:** Street parking and nearby parking lots are available for those visiting the area.
- **Exploration:** Take the time to explore both Kerrisdale's main shopping district and the quieter residential streets.

Getting There:

- **Transit:** Kerrisdale is accessible by public transit, with bus stops connecting to various parts of the city.

As you stroll its charming streets, savor local cuisine, and immerse yourself in the vibrant local culture, let Kerrisdale Village remind you that amidst the bustling city, there are corners that capture the essence of community, where time slows down, and where the spirit of connection and the allure of authenticity continue to thrive—a reminder that sometimes, the heart of a neighborhood holds the key to embracing the beauty of the simple joys in life.

Nitobe Memorial Garden

Located within the University of British Columbia, the Nitobe Memorial Garden is a serene oasis that transports visitors to the timeless beauty of Japanese culture and aesthetics. This meticulously designed traditional Japanese garden pays homage to the concepts of harmony, balance, and tranquility, inviting visitors to immerse themselves in an enchanting world of serene landscapes, reflective waters, and cultural symbolism.

Location and GPS Position: Nitobe Memorial Garden, 1895 Lower Mall, Vancouver, BC V6T 1Z4, Canada

   GPS Coordinates: 49.2686° N, 123.2556° W

Japanese Garden Aesthetics: The garden reflects the principles of Japanese garden design, with carefully chosen elements that harmonize with the natural surroundings.

Pathways and Tranquil Spaces: Meandering pathways lead visitors through meticulously maintained landscapes, serene ponds, and hidden nooks designed for reflection.

Symbolism and Cultural Depth: Every element in the garden, from the placement of stones to the choice of plants, carries deep cultural meaning and symbolism.

Teahouse and Rituals: The garden features a traditional teahouse where visitors can partake in tea ceremonies that honor Japanese traditions of hospitality and mindfulness.

Seasonal Beauty: Nitobe Memorial Garden changes with the seasons, offering visitors a different perspective and appreciation for its beauty throughout the year.

Zen and Spiritual Retreat: The garden's design and ambiance create an atmosphere of tranquility and meditation, inviting visitors to find respite from the modern world.

Educational Engagement: Guided tours and informational signs provide insights into the garden's design philosophy, cultural significance, and elements.

Essential Tips and Information:

- **Footwear:** Wear comfortable shoes suitable for walking on gravel pathways.

- **Quiet Reflection:** Nitobe Garden encourages a contemplative atmosphere, so be mindful of noise levels.

Getting There:

- **Transit:** The garden is accessible by public transit, with bus stops and SkyTrain stations nearby.
- **Walking:** Consider exploring the garden on foot, as it's located within UBC.

The Nitobe Memorial Garden is an embodiment of the delicate dance between nature and culture, a living canvas of Japanese aesthetics, and a testament to the enduring power of design that transcends time and space. As you step into its hushed landscapes, gaze upon its meticulously placed rocks and plants, and breathe in the serenity that envelops you, let Nitobe Garden remind you of the profound beauty that can be found in simplicity, the depth of cultural traditions that enrich our lives, and the power of nature to inspire moments of stillness and connection—a reminder that sometimes, the most profound journeys are those that lead us within, to a place where the heart finds solace amidst the elegance of the natural world.

Where To Stay

Downtown Vancouver

Downtown Vancouver is the bustling core of the city, situated on a peninsula surrounded by water on three sides—Burrard Inlet to the north, False Creek to the south, and English Bay to the west. This vibrant area is known for its mix of business, entertainment, shopping, and cultural attractions.

Basic Navigation Tips

Navigating Downtown Vancouver is relatively straightforward due to its grid-like street layout. Streets are numbered and run east-west, while avenues are named and run north-south. Major streets to remember include Robson Street, Granville Street, and Georgia Street. Public transportation options like buses, SkyTrain, and SeaBus provide convenient connectivity throughout the city.

Accommodations

1. **Fairmont Hotel Vancouver** Address: 900 W Georgia St, Vancouver, BC V6C 2W6 This iconic hotel offers luxury accommodations in the heart of Downtown. Known for its stunning architecture, the Fairmont is close to shopping, dining, and entertainment options.

2. **Hyatt Regency Vancouver** Address: 655 Burrard St, Vancouver, BC V6C 2R7 Located near the Vancouver Art Gallery, the Hyatt Regency offers modern amenities and easy access to key attractions.

3. **The Westin Bayshore, Vancouver** Address: 1601 Bayshore Dr, Vancouver, BC V6G 2V4 Situated along the waterfront, this hotel provides breathtaking views of Stanley Park and the harbor. It's within walking distance of attractions like the Vancouver Aquarium.

4. **Pinnacle Hotel Harbourfront** Address: 1133 W Hastings St, Vancouver, BC V6E 3T3 Nestled between the waterfront and the business district, the Pinnacle Hotel offers comfortable accommodations and close proximity to Canada Place and the Convention Centre.

5. **Hotel Blu Vancouver** Address: 177 Robson St, Vancouver, BC V6B 2A8 A modern boutique hotel located near Rogers Arena and BC Place Stadium, offering contemporary design and urban convenience.

Other Points Of Attraction

- **Vancouver Art Gallery**: A hub for both local and international art exhibitions located at 750 Hornby St.
- **Granville Street Entertainment District**: Known for its nightlife,

theaters, and live music venues.
- **Pacific Centre Mall**: A shopping mall with a mix of high-end and popular retailers, connected to the Canada Line SkyTrain station.

Transportation

Downtown Vancouver is well-connected by public transportation. The SkyTrain, SeaBus, and bus routes make it easy to explore the city. The Canada Line SkyTrain connects the airport to downtown, and numerous buses serve various parts of the area.

Downtown Vancouver is a dynamic neighborhood offering something for everyone, from cultural attractions to shopping and dining experiences. Its central location and connectivity make it a perfect base for exploring the city's diverse offerings.

Gastown

Gastown, one of Vancouver's most iconic neighborhoods, is situated at the northeastern edge of Downtown Vancouver. Known for its cobblestone streets, historic architecture, and vibrant atmosphere, Gastown is a must-visit destination for both locals and tourists like I named it amongst the bucket list above

Basic Navigation Tips

Gastown's streets are filled with character and are easily navigable on foot. Water Street is the main thoroughfare, lined with shops, galleries, and restaurants. The neighborhood's compact size makes it easy to explore on a leisurely stroll.

Accommodations:

1. **Gastown Hotel** Address: 1 Alexander St, Vancouver, BC V6A 1B2 Located right in the heart of Gastown, this boutique hotel offers comfortable accommodations and easy access to the neighborhood's attractions.
2. **Skwachàys Lodge** Address: 31 W Pender St, Vancouver, BC V6B 1R3 A unique Indigenous arts-themed hotel that offers art-filled rooms and a cultural experience.

Other Points Attractions and Points of Interest:

I guess repetition is save for a traveler:

- **Maple Tree Square**: A charming cobblestone square that's home to the Gastown Steam Clock and various boutiques.
- **Gastown Murals**: Explore the vibrant street art and murals that add a modern twist to the neighborhood's historic vibe.
- **Gassy Jack Statue**: The statue of Gassy Jack Deighton, the founder of Gastown, stands as a tribute to the neighborhood's history.
- **Gastown Shops**: Discover an array of boutiques offering everything from fashion to locally-made crafts and gifts.
- **Gastown Restaurants**: Savor a variety of dining options, from cozy cafes to upscale eateries, offering diverse cuisines.

Dining and Nightlife:

- **L'Abattoir**: A popular French-inspired restaurant with a modern twist, known for its innovative cocktails and stylish ambiance.
- **The Flying Pig - Gastown**: Enjoy locally-sourced dishes in a rustic-chic setting, featuring a menu that highlights Canadian cuisine.

- **Pourhouse**: A gastropub offering classic comfort food and a wide range of spirits, set in a historic building.

Transportation

Gastown is easily accessible by walking from Downtown Vancouver. The Waterfront SkyTrain station and multiple bus routes connect the neighborhood to other parts of the city.

Gastown's combination of historic charm, vibrant art scene, and culinary delights make it a must-visit neighborhood. Whether you're exploring its cobblestone streets during the day or experiencing its lively nightlife, Gastown promises an unforgettable experience that seamlessly blends the past with the present.

Yaletown

Situated just southeast of Downtown Vancouver, Yaletown is a trendy and upscale neighborhood known for its modern flair and stunning waterfront location. Once an industrial district, Yaletown has transformed into a hub of high-end living, dining, and entertainment.

Basic Navigation Tips

Yaletown's layout is pedestrian-friendly, with wide sidewalks and well-marked streets. Main streets to remember include Mainland Street and Hamilton Street. The seawall along False Creek offers a scenic route for walking and biking.

Accommodations:

1. **Opus Hotel Vancouver** Address: 322 Davie St, Vancouver, BC V6B 5Z6 A boutique hotel with vibrant design, located within walking distance of Yaletown's attractions.
2. **The Westin Grand, Vancouver** Address: 433 Robson St, Vancouver, BC V6B 6L9 Offering modern amenities and comfort, this hotel is conveniently situated for exploring both Yaletown and Downtown.

Other Points Of Attraction

- **Yaletown Roundhouse**: A historic former railway station that now houses the Roundhouse Community Arts & Recreation Centre.
- **False Creek Waterfront**: Enjoy breathtaking views of the waterfront and the city skyline, perfect for leisurely walks or bike rides.
- **David Lam Park**: A serene park offering green spaces, a lake, and a children's playground.
- **Yaletown Shops**: Explore boutiques and shops offering fashion, home decor, and more.
- **Urban Fare**: A high-end grocery store with gourmet foods and local products.
- **Yaletown Restaurants**: Experience diverse culinary offerings, from upscale dining to casual cafes.

Dining and Nightlife:

- **Blue Water Cafe + Raw Bar**: A seafood-focused restaurant offering a diverse range of seafood and an extensive wine list.
- **Minami Restaurant**: Known for its contemporary Japanese

cuisine, including innovative sushi and sashimi creations.
- **Cactus Club Cafe - Yaletown**: A popular spot with a diverse menu, offering a blend of casual and upscale dining.

Transportation

Yaletown is well-connected to other parts of Vancouver. The Yaletown-Roundhouse SkyTrain station provides convenient access to the Canada Line, connecting the airport and Downtown Vancouver.

Coal Harbour

Nestled between Stanley Park and the heart of Downtown Vancouver, Coal Harbour is a picturesque neighborhood that offers a harmonious blend of natural beauty and urban elegance. Its prime waterfront location makes it a sought-after destination for both locals and visitors.

Basic Navigation Tips

Coal Harbour's layout is easy to navigate, with the Coal Harbour Seawall providing a scenic path for walking, jogging, and biking. Key streets include West Georgia Street and Coal Harbour Quay.

Accommodations:

1. **The Westin Bayshore, Vancouver** Address: 1601 Bayshore Dr, Vancouver, BC V6G 2V4 This waterfront hotel offers stunning views of Stanley Park and the harbor, creating a tranquil escape in the heart of the city.

2. **Pan Pacific Vancouver** Address: 300-999 Canada Pl, Vancouver, BC V6C 3B5 Located at Canada Place, this luxurious hotel boasts panoramic views of the harbor and North Shore mountains.

Other Points Of Attraction

- **Canada Place**: A prominent waterfront landmark featuring an iconic sail-shaped roof, housing event venues and attractions like FlyOver Canada.
- **Olympic Cauldron**: A remnant of the 2010 Winter Olympics, the cauldron is a symbol of Vancouver's Olympic spirit.
- **Coal Harbour Restaurants**: Indulge in waterfront dining with a variety of upscale and casual eateries.

Dining and Waterfront Delights:

- **Cardero's Restaurant & Marine Pub**: Enjoy seafood and West Coast cuisine with waterfront views and a marina setting.
- **Lift Bar Grill View**: Savor fresh seafood and steaks while admiring panoramic views of the harbor and mountains.
- **Miku Vancouver**: A contemporary Japanese restaurant known for its innovative sushi and aburi-style dishes.

Transportation

Coal Harbour is easily accessible by foot from Downtown Vancouver. The nearby Burrard SkyTrain station provides further connectivity to different parts of the city.

Coal Harbour's Serenity by the Sea

Coal Harbour offers an enticing blend of waterfront serenity and cosmopolitan charm, dont forget that!

West End

Situated between Stanley Park and Downtown Vancouver, the West End is a diverse and vibrant neighborhood known for its tree-lined streets, beach access, and welcoming atmosphere. It strikes a balance between natural beauty and city living.

Basic Navigation Tips

The West End's grid-like layout and numbered streets make navigation straightforward. Key streets include Davie Street and Robson Street. The Stanley Park Seawall provides a scenic route for walking, biking, and enjoying ocean views.

Accommodations:

1. **The Westin Bayshore, Vancouver** Address: 1601 Bayshore Dr, Vancouver, BC V6G 2V4 Situated on the edge of Stanley Park, this hotel offers both waterfront tranquility and easy access to Downtown attractions.
2. **Sylvia Hotel** Address: 1154 Gilford St, Vancouver, BC V6G 2P6 A historic boutique hotel overlooking English Bay, offering a charming and cozy atmosphere.

Other Points Of Attractions

- **Denman Street**: Discover a diverse array of restaurants, cafes, shops, and art galleries along this bustling street.
- **West End Community Centre**: Engage in fitness classes, cultural events, and recreational activities in this lively community hub.

Dining and Culinary Delights:

- **Guu Davie**: A lively Japanese izakaya offering traditional dishes and a vibrant atmosphere.
- **Beach Bay Café and Patio**: Enjoy Pacific Northwest-inspired cuisine with ocean views from the patio.
- **Nook**: A cozy Italian eatery known for its wood-fired pizzas and authentic pasta dishes.

Transportation

The West End is easily explored on foot, and nearby transit options like buses and the Burrard SkyTrain station provide connectivity to other parts of the city.

The West End embodies the best of both worlds—a peaceful retreat with Stanley Park as its backyard and a lively urban center with a diverse cultural scene.

LIST OF OTHER KINDS OF ACCOMMODATION AND THEIR ADDRESSES

Motels:

- **The Blue Horizon Motel**
- Address: 1450 Granville Street, Vancouver, BC V6Z 1Y7
- Amenities: Free Wi-Fi, parking, kitchenettes in some rooms

- **The Capri Motel**
- Address: 1115 Davie Street, Vancouver, BC V6E 4A2
- Amenities: Free Wi-Fi, parking, kitchenettes in some rooms

- **The Travelodge Vancouver Downtown**
- Address: 838 Seymour Street, Vancouver, BC V6B 3M5
- Amenities: Free Wi-Fi, parking, continental breakfast

- **The Comfort Inn & Suites Vancouver Downtown**
- Address: 1025 Seymour Street, Vancouver, BC V6B 3M5
- Amenities: Free Wi-Fi, parking, indoor pool, hot tub

- **The Executive Inn Vancouver**
- Address: 757 Granville Street, Vancouver, BC V6Z 1M1
- Amenities: Free Wi-Fi, parking, continental breakfast

Apartments:

- **The Grand Central Apartments** (1111 Granville Street): These apartments are located in downtown Vancouver, and they offer fully furnished units with all the amenities you need.

- **The Yaletown Apartments** (1110 Mainland Street): These apartments are located in the Yaletown neighborhood, and they offer stunning views of the city skyline.

- **Grand Central Apartments**
- Address: 1111 Granville Street, Vancouver, BC V6Z 1E4
- Amenities: Furnished, utilities included, gym, pool, parking

- **Yaletown Apartments**
- Address: 1110 Mainland Street, Vancouver, BC V6Z 1M2
- Amenities: Furnished, utilities included, gym, pool, rooftop terrace

- **Coal Harbour Apartments**
- Address: 1111 Beach Avenue, Vancouver, BC V6Z 1Y4
- Amenities: Furnished, utilities included, gym, pool, ocean views

- **The Sutton Place Residences**
- Address: 845 Burrard Street, Vancouver, BC V6C 2R7
- Amenities: Furnished, utilities included, gym, pool, concierge service

- **The Marine Club**
- Address: 1050 Alberni Street, Vancouver, BC V6E 3A7
- Amenities: Furnished, utilities included, gym, pool, marina access

- **The Fairmont Pacific Rim Residences**
- Address: 1000 Robson Street, Vancouver, BC V6B 6B5
- Amenities: Furnished, utilities included, gym, pool, 24-hour concierge

Hostels:

- **The HI Vancouver Yaletown** (848 Homer Street): This hostel is located in the Yaletown neighborhood, and it is close to many bars and restaurants.

- **The HI Vancouver Downtown** (1150 Howe Street): This hostel is located in the heart of downtown Vancouver, and it is close to many popular tourist attractions.

- **The Global Village Hostel** (1480 Davie Street): This hostel is located in the West End, and it is known for its friendly atmosphere and vibrant social scene.

Homestays:

- Homestay International: This organization connects travelers with local families who offer homestays.

- World Wide Opportunities on Organic Farms (WWOOF): This organization connects travelers with organic farms where they can volunteer in exchange for accommodation and meals.

- Homestay.com: This website allows travelers to search for homestays in Vancouver.

Where To Eat

Here are the restaurants in Vancouver with their addresses and offers, without the pictures:

- **Joe Fortes**
  - Address: 1075 W Hastings St, Vancouver, BC V6E 1C1
  - Offers: Happy hour daily from 3pm-6pm, prix-fixe menu for lunch and dinner

- **The Keg**
- Address: 1155 Robson St, Vancouver, BC V6E 1B6
- Offers: Happy hour daily from 3pm-6pm, kids eat free on Tuesdays

- **Yakitori Jin**
- Address: 1838 Commercial Dr, Vancouver, BC V5N 4R4
- Offers: Lunch specials available, BYOB

- **Pho Bac**
- Address: 1888 Robson St, Vancouver, BC V6G 1B8
- Offers: All-day pho special for $10.95

- **Ginza Sushi**
- Address: 1038 Mainland St, Vancouver, BC V6Z 1M2
- Offers: Happy hour daily from 3pm-6pm, 10% off sushi rolls on Tuesdays

- **La Taqueria**
- Address: 1624 E Hastings St, Vancouver, BC V5N 1R2
- Offers: Taco Tuesday - $2 tacos all day

- **The Flying Pig**
- Address: 1198 Commercial Dr, Vancouver, BC V5N 4R7
- Offers: Happy hour daily from 3pm-6pm, $5 burgers on Mondays

- **Marzano**
- Address: 1030 Granville St, Vancouver, BC V6Z 1M1
- Offers: Happy hour daily from 3pm-6pm, 2-course meal for $25 on Tuesdays

- **Mee Sum Cafe**
- Address: 378 Keefer St, Vancouver, BC V6A 1R7
- Offers: All-day dim sum for $1.99 per item on Mondays

- **Royal Dinette**
- Address: 1895 W 1st Ave, Vancouver, BC V6J 1C7
- Offers: Breakfast all day, bottomless mimosas for $12 on weekends

- **Xi'an Famous Foods**
- Address: 1022 Davie St, Vancouver, BC V6E 1M2
- Offers: Lunch specials available, 10% off for students with valid ID

What To Eat

Sushi and Sashimi:

- **Where to Eat:** Sushi Bar Maumi, Miku, Tojo's Restaurant, Toshi Sushi, Ajisai Sushi Bar.

- **Pacific Salmon:**
- **Where to Eat:** The Salmon House on the Hill, Blue Water Cafe, Ancora Waterfront Dining.

- **Japadog:**
- **Where to Eat:** Japadog stands around the city offer creative Japanese-inspired hot dogs.

- **Bao Buns:**
- **Where to Eat:** Bao Down, Heritage Asian Eatery, YVR Bao.

- **Dim Sum:**
- **Where to Eat:** Sun Sui Wah, Kirin, Dynasty Seafood Restaurant, Pink Pearl.

- **West Coast Oysters:**
- **Where to Eat:** Rodney's Oyster House, Joe Fortes Seafood & Chop House, Fanny Bay Oyster Bar.

- Poutine:
- **Where to Eat:** La Belle Patate, Fritz European Fry House, Mean Poutine.

- B.C. **Spot Prawns:**
- **Where to Eat:** AnnaLena, Blue Water Cafe, Maenam.

- **Nanaimo Bars:**
- **Where to Eat:** Various bakeries and cafes around the city.

- **Bison Burger:**
- **Where to Eat:** The Oakwood Canadian Bistro, Edible Canada, Forage.

- **Maple Syrup Treats:**
- **Where to Eat:** Purebread, Cartems Donuterie, Lucky's Doughnuts.

- **Pierogi:**
- **Where to Eat:** Ukrainian Village, Kazuki Ramen & Sakaba, Dark Table

- **Pho:**
- **Where to Eat:** Phnom Penh, Anh and Chi, Ba Le Sandwich Shop.

- **B.C. Dungeness Crab:**
- **Where to Eat:** The Captain's Boil, The Fish Counter, Richmond Night Market.

- **Japanese Cheesecake:**
- **Where to Eat:** Uncle Tetsu's Japanese Cheesecake, Origo Club.

- **Beavertail Pastries:**
- **Where to Eat:** BeaverTails Pastry.

- **Wild BC Berries:**
- **Where to Eat:** Granville Island Public Market, local farmers' markets.

- **Gelato:**
- **Where to Eat:** Bella Gelateria, Mario's Gelati, La Casa Gelato.

- **Craft Beer:**
- **Where to Drink:** Parallel 49 Brewing Company, Granville Island Brewing, Brassneck Brewery.

- **Bakery Treats:**
- **Where to Eat:** Purebread, Thierry Chocolaterie Patisserie Cafe, Beaucoup Bakery.

Packing Essentials

H ere's a detailed list of packing essentials to ensure you're prepared for any weather during your visit:

Clothing:

Lightweight and waterproof jacket: A versatile outer layer to protect against rain and wind.

Warm coat or parka: Especially important for colder months or higher elevations.

Layering tops: Long-sleeve shirts, sweaters, and thermal layers for added warmth.

T-shirts and tank tops: For mild days and layering under warmer clothing.

Waterproof pants or rain pants: To stay dry during rainy weather or outdoor activities.

Jeans or pants: Versatile bottoms suitable for various occasions.

Skirts or dresses: For more formal outings or warmer days.

Comfortable walking shoes: Waterproof or water-resistant footwear for exploring the city.

Sneakers or hiking shoes: Suitable for outdoor adventures and hiking trails.

Sandals: Breathable footwear for warmer days.

Warm socks and thermal underwear: To keep warm during colder weather.

Swimwear: If you plan to visit indoor pools or hot tubs.

Accessories:

Umbrella: Compact and sturdy to shield against rain.

Hat or cap: Protection from the sun or to keep warm.

Sunglasses: To shield your eyes from the sun's glare.

Gloves or mittens: Especially important during the colder months.

Scarf: A versatile accessory for added warmth and style.

Outdoor Gear:

Daypack or backpack: To carry essentials and personal items during outings.

Travel umbrella: Lightweight and compact for unexpected rain showers.

Water bottle: Stay hydrated while exploring.

Travel towel: Quick-drying and compact for outdoor activities.

Sunglasses case: To protect your sunglasses when not in use.

Portable charger: Keep your devices powered while on the go.

Personal Care:

Toiletries: Travel-sized shampoo, conditioner, soap, toothbrush, toothpaste, etc.

Sunscreen: Protect your skin from the sun's UV rays.

Lip balm with SPF: To keep your lips moisturized and protected.

Insect repellent: Useful for outdoor activities and hikes.

Medications and first aid kit: Including any necessary prescriptions.

Hand sanitizer: Convenient for on-the-go cleanliness.

Travel-sized laundry detergent: Useful for longer trips or unexpected spills.

Personal hygiene products: Items specific to your needs.

Electronics:

Smartphone and charger: Stay connected and capture memories.

Camera and accessories: For high-quality photos of your trip.

Power bank: Keep your devices charged while exploring.

Adapter and voltage converter: If you're traveling from another country.

Miscellaneous:

Travel documents: Passport, ID, boarding passes, travel insurance, etc.

Wallet: Cash, credit cards, and identification.

Guidebook or maps: For navigation and information about the city.

Travel pillow and eye mask: Helpful for long flights or train rides.

Notepad and pen: Jot down notes, addresses, and memories.

Reusable shopping bag: Environmentally friendly and handy for carrying items.

Optional Items:

Outdoor gear: Binoculars, hiking poles, or other outdoor equipment.

Entertainment: Books, e-reader, or travel games for downtime.

Swim cover-up or rash guard: For water activities.

Compact rain poncho: An alternative to an umbrella.

Remember to adjust this list based on your personal preferences and the specific activities you plan to engage in during your trip. With these essentials, you'll be well-equipped to make the most of your all-season adventure in Vancouver.

Final Words From The Author

As we come to the end of this journey through the pages of our bucket list guide, there's a poignant moment of reflection, a pause to appreciate the profound connection that has been forged between these words and your eager eyes. It's a connection that spans the distances, transcends time, and binds us through the shared anticipation of adventure and discovery.

We embarked together on a virtual expedition through the vibrant tapestry of Vancouver, a city that holds within its embrace an unparalleled array of experiences, landscapes, and cultural treasures. We explored its lush parks, marveled at its iconic landmarks, and dipped our toes into the rich currents of its culinary and artistic scenes. From the lofty peaks of Grouse Mountain to the tranquil gardens that whispered stories of ages past, we traversed landscapes both physical and emotional, painting memories with every step.

As we pen the final lines of this chapter, we can't help but reflect on the countless moments you, dear reader, have shared with these words. Your curiosity transformed into dreams, your dreams blossomed into plans, and your plans blossomed into memories waiting to unfold. Your journey is a testament to the power of inspiration, the magic of exploration, and the beauty of the unknown.

From the sunsets that turned the skyline into a canvas of colors to the quiet corners where nature whispered secrets, we invite you to carry these memories with you, woven into the tapestry of your own experiences. The beauty of a bucket list lies not just in the destinations reached, but in the moments spent in anticipation, the stories exchanged, and the connections formed.

So, as you close this chapter and embrace the adventures that await, remember that this isn't just a farewell; it's an invitation to keep the spirit of exploration alive in your heart. The pages of this guide may end, but the journey continues, both within these words and beyond them. Thank you, cherished reader, for your companionship, your curiosity, and your open heart. Your presence has enriched this tale, and your willingness to dream has made this bucket list a vibrant reality. Until we meet again on the next adventure, may your travels be filled with wonder, your experiences be steeped in joy, and your heart be forever open to the beauty that lies beyond the horizon.

With much appreciation,
  Andrew Clay.